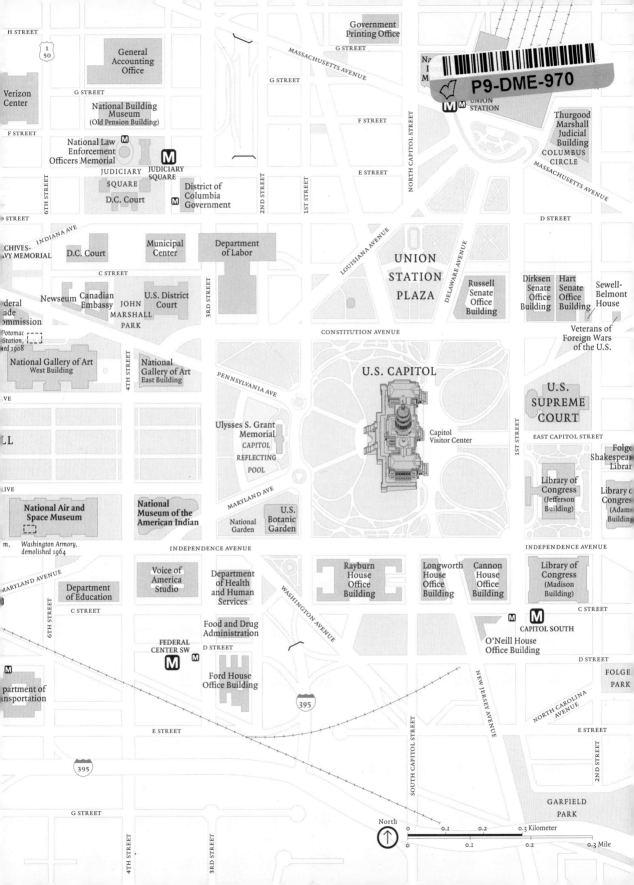

H STREET

General Accounting Office

Verizon Center

G STREET

National Building Museum
(Old Pension Building)

F STREET

National Law Enforcement Officers Memorial

Ⓜ

JUDICIARY SQUARE

Ⓜ JUDICIARY SQUARE

D.C. Court

District of Columbia Government

Government Printing Office

G STREET

MASSACHUSETTS AVENUE

G STREET

F STREET

E STREET

Na
I
M

P9-DME-970

Ⓜ Ⓜ UNION STATION

Thurgood Marshall Judicial Building

COLUMBUS CIRCLE

MASSACHUSETTS AVENUE

D STREET

...CHIVES-
...VY MEMORIAL

INDIANA AVE

D.C. Court

Municipal Center

Department of Labor

C STREET

Newseum

Canadian Embassy

JOHN MARSHALL PARK

U.S. District Court

...deral
...ade
...mmission

Potomac
Station,
...ed 1908

National Gallery of Art West Building

National Gallery of Art East Building

...VE

...LL

...IVE

National Air and Space Museum

...m,   Washington Armory,
demolished 1964

MARYLAND AVENUE

Department of Education

C STREET

FEDERAL CENTER SW

Ⓜ Ⓜ

Department of Transportation

Ⓜ

6TH STREET

G STREET

4TH STREET

3RD STREET

2ND STREET

1ST STREET

LOUISIANA AVENUE

DELAWARE AVENUE

UNION STATION PLAZA

Russell Senate Office Building

Dirksen Senate Office Building

Hart Senate Office Building

Sewell-Belmont House

CONSTITUTION AVENUE

Veterans of Foreign Wars of the U.S.

PENNSYLVANIA AVE

U.S. CAPITOL

Ulysses S. Grant Memorial

CAPITOL REFLECTING POOL

Capitol Visitor Center

U.S. SUPREME COURT

EAST CAPITOL STREET

1ST STREET

Folge
Shakespea
Librar

Library of Congress (Jefferson Building)

Library c
Congress
(Adams
Building

MARYLAND AVE

National Museum of the American Indian

National Garden

U.S. Botanic Garden

INDEPENDENCE AVENUE

INDEPENDENCE AVENUE

Voice of America Studio

Department of Health and Human Services

Food and Drug Administration

D STREET

Ford House Office Building

WASHINGTON AVENUE

Rayburn House Office Building

Longworth House Office Building

Cannon House Office Building

Library of Congress (Madison Building)

C STREET

Ⓜ Ⓜ CAPITOL SOUTH

O'Neill House Office Building

D STREET

FOLGE
PARK

395

NEW JERSEY AVENUE

NORTH CAROLINA AVENUE

E STREET

E STREET

2ND STREET

SOUTH CAPITOL STREET

395

GARFIELD PARK

North

↑

0   0.1   0.2   0.3 Kilometer

0   0.1   0.2   0.3 Mile

A GUIDE TO SMITHSONIAN
ARCHITECTURE

Heather Ewing and Amy Ballard · Smithsonian Books · Washington

Funding for this book was provided by the
Smithsonian Women's Committee and the
Office of Planning and Project Management.

Prepared by the Office of Architectural
History and Historic Preservation,
Smithsonian Institution

Edited by Diane Maddex, Archetype Press

Designed by Robert L. Wiser

Library of Congress
Cataloging-in-Publication Data

Ewing, Heather P.
A guide to Smithsonian architecture / by
Heather Ewing and Amy Ballard. — 1st ed.
      p.   cm.
Includes bibliographical references.
ISBN 978-1-58834-261-4 (pbk.)
1. Smithsonian Institution—Buildings.
2. Museum buildings—United States.
3. Architecture—United States.
4. Research institutes—United States.
I. Ballard, Amy. II. Title.
NA6751.E95 2008
727'.60009753—dc22

                              2008033587

First Edition

14 13 12 11 10 09   5 4 3 2 1

Printed in China

All illustrations in this book are from the
collections of the Smithsonian Institution,
except for the following:

Endpapers: Peter Penczer and the National
Park Service; pages 8–9: Skidmore, Owings
and Merrill (© Eduard Hueber, 2008/Arch-
photo.com); page 15 top: National Archives;
page 18: Historic American Buildings Survey,
Library of Congress: page 19: Library of
Congress; page 25: National Archives; page 27
top: National Archives; page 30: Bettman/
Corbis; page 98: Ezra Stoller © Esto;
page 100: Skidmore, Owings and Merrill
(© Eduard Hueber, 2008/archphoto.com).

Most of the contemporary photographs were
taken by the Smithsonian's photographers,
including Ken Rahaim and Eric Long.
Please see page 154 for acknowledgments of
additional staff members who assisted with
the photographs and other illustrations.

Endpapers: Map of the National Mall,
showing many of the Smithsonian's museums
and other national landmarks.

Page 1: A mosaic of the Smithsonian seal
(1893, Augustus Saint-Gaudens), located at the
entrance to the Regents' Room in the Castle.

Pages 2–3: The final stone of the Natural
History Museum's south portico being laid on
May 11, 1909. The museum's neoclassical
style contrasts with the medieval character of
the Castle, seen across the Mall.

Page 160: A drawing of James Smithson's
neoclassical marble sarcophagus, made
in Genoa, Italy. Located in the Castle crypt,
it is embellished with funerary ornamenta-
tion, such as the pine-cone finial at the top,
symbolizing regeneration.

CONTENTS

FOREWORD

When the Smithsonian Castle, the institution's first building, opened in 1855, it stood virtually alone on what is now the National Mall. Today our buildings— from science laboratories to sprawling architectural treasures rich in history— are dispersed around the globe. Reflecting the Smithsonian's diversified mission and important position as the world's largest museum and research complex, its mixture of museums, science facilities, libraries, and conservation centers is a wonder to behold. Having seen consuming fires, inaugural balls, and frequent change, our buildings tell an important part of the Smithsonian's development but also speak to the larger narrative of American history.

As a visitor over the years, I have been intrigued by the widely divergent styles of the Smithsonian's museums but had no reference that would explain what I was seeing. This engaging book, documenting the major buildings that make up the institution today, fills that gap. We learn here that these structures trace the arc of American architecture, some designed to display art and historical artifacts, others built to house scientific collections and laboratories.

We are fortunate that the team of Heather Ewing and Amy Ballard chose to undertake this book. The two are especially qualified for the task: Heather Ewing wrote *The Lost World of James Smithson* and is a research associate of the Smithsonian Archives, while Amy Ballard is the senior historic preservation specialist in our Office of Architectural History and Historic Preservation.

Our buildings serve millions of visitors, who are welcomed every day except Christmas. But they must also meet the needs of scholars, curators, and scientists who work behind the scenes, carrying out the institution's mission. Ms. Ewing and Ms. Ballard eloquently demonstrate that somehow it all works.

As an engineer, I appreciate the drama and the challenges that each building project involves and commend the authors for conveying the human stories within the buildings. Such a human dimension helps us appreciate the genius behind the architecture and demonstrates anew how a building serves as an embodiment of ideas. This book opened my eyes to the long history, broad range, and architectural significance of the Smithsonian's buildings. I hope that it will do the same for you.

G. Wayne Clough, Secretary
Smithsonian Institution

In the late nineteenth century, the Castle's north carriage porch (opposite) looked out onto what was then the picturesque Smithsonian Park. After 1901 the McMillan Commission returned this area to the classical plan envisioned by Pierre Charles L'Enfant.

Pages 8–9: The McMillan Plan of 1901 envisioned the Mall lined with monumental museums. Today the red sandstone towers of the Castle on the south and the Beaux-Arts dome of the Natural History Museum on the north are focal points of this important public space.

PREFACE

THE LARGEST COLLECTION

Many visitors to Washington, D.C., think that most, if not all, of the Smithsonian museums are located on the National Mall and downtown. But there is much more to the Smithsonian than its buildings in the heart of the capital. On a daily basis, the institution actually takes care of more than seven hundred properties in locations from nearby Maryland and Virginia to New York City, Massachusetts, and Florida, and farther afield to Arizona, Hawaii, Belize, and Panama.

The stewardship of what can be called the Smithsonian's largest collection—its buildings—has been an ongoing concern since the first section of its first building, now known as the Castle, opened in 1849. However, it was not until 1880 that the institution's first superintendent of buildings, Henry Horan, was named. He held the post until 1896, when the Division of Buildings and Superintendence was created. With the Smithsonian's growth, this division has undergone several name changes and reorganizations. Now the Office of Facilities, Engineering and Operations, it is responsible for the daily care and maintenance of the Smithsonian's buildings and grounds. Under its umbrella are most of the institution's support services: security, safety, health and environmental management, facilities management (maintenance), geospatial, horticulture, project management, planning, architectural history and historic preservation, real estate, design, and engineering and construction. Its staff of more than 1,700 employees works mostly behind the scenes to protect, maintain, and curate the Smithsonian's architectural heritage.

In addition to encompassing and exhibiting impressive collections, the buildings of the Smithsonian themselves serve as icons of great cultural significance. Their forms illustrate changing styles and sensibilities, documenting America's growth as a nation. Each one represents a specific time in history: the turreted Castle reflects the eclectic Victorian era, the majestically domed National Museum of Natural History illustrates the neoclassical leanings of the turn of the twentieth century, the glass-filled National Air and Space Museum recalls the spare modernism of the 1970s, and the expressionistic National Museum of the American Indian has helped launch the Smithsonian architecturally into the twenty-first century.

Many of the Smithsonian's buildings are National Historic Landmarks or are included in the National Register of Historic Places, the official roster of the nation's historic properties, sites, districts, structures, objects, and landmarks.

More than 80,000 sites in the United States are listed in the National Register, and 2,400 are National Historic Landmarks. The institution is proud that several of its buildings carry these designations, which are deemed by the secretary of the interior to have exceptional value to the nation.

In 1993 the Architectural History and Historic Preservation Office developed a historic preservation policy for the Smithsonian, outlining the institution's commitment to protect and preserve the buildings and sites in its care. Every design and construction project initiated by the institution follows recommended guidelines entitled the Secretary of the Interior's Standards and Guidelines for the Treatment of Historic Properties. Public and private owners of historic properties use these standards throughout the United States to ensure sound preservation methodology for projects large and small.

This guide presents the Smithsonian's buildings in the order in which they were built or acquired by the institution, beginning with the Castle and ending with the National Museum of the American Indian. When a site includes distinct but intertwined facilities, all are discussed together under the main museum listing. At the end of the book are grouped less visible but no less important structures, the institution's research centers and support facilities. For readers interested in a strictly architectural chronology of the Smithsonian's buildings, which actually begins with Robert Mills's Patent Office Building of 1836 (today the home of the Smithsonian American Art Museum and the National Portrait Gallery), there is a chronology at the back of the book.

In 1964, shortly after becoming the Smithsonian's eighth secretary, S. Dillon Ripley observed that "the facilities and resources at the Smithsonian are tremendous . . . yet with the phenomenal growth of the Smithsonian have come almost awe-inspiring opportunities and challenges." These words hold true today and no doubt will in the future, as the Smithsonian expands its collection of buildings with the National Museum of African American History and Culture and continues to care for its architectural legacy. Although the Smithsonian is the caretaker of these buildings, it holds them in trust on your behalf. We invite you to explore these treasures and experience our collective history through its largest collection.

Heather Ewing and Amy Ballard

Pages 10–11: A rose window is a prominent feature of the Castle's west end. Two other rose windows can be found on the west side of the third-floor library and on the north facade.

An 1881 engraving of James Smithson, who bequeathed his estate to establish the Smithsonian Institution, is based on a miniature by Henri Johns (painted in France in 1816).

"The name of Smithson is not to be transmitted to posterity by a monument of brick and mortar, but by the effects of his institution on his fellow men." So wrote Joseph Henry (1797–1878), the first secretary of the Smithsonian, a month after Congress passed the legislation establishing the Smithsonian Institution in August 1846. There had been much debate over the bequest of James Smithson (ca. 1765–1829), which called for the creation in Washington of "an establishment for the increase and diffusion of knowledge among men." Some wondered why an English scientist who had never set foot in the United States would leave it his fortune (more than a half million dollars in the 1830s), and many questioned what exactly an institution for the increase and diffusion of knowledge should be— a national library, a university, a museum, an astrophysical observatory, a teacher training college? The act of Congress included a little bit of everything, and some members of the Board of Regents, the governing body for the new Smithsonian, believed that a grand and symbolic building to house all of these functions would establish the new institution's place in the nation's capital.

Joseph Henry, America's foremost scientist in the nineteenth century, thought instead that Smithson's extraordinary gift should be devoted to original scientific research. He saw in the idea of the Smithsonian the opportunity to place the United States on a scientific footing equal to that of Europe. The way to perpetuate Smithson's name, Henry reasoned, was to build a community of scientists, support their work, and disseminate their discoveries through a system of publications. In fact, his vision did become a reality. The scientific work of the Smithsonian, although little known to the public, is a critically important part of its mission. Today the institution runs scientific stations and research programs around the world, including a global volcanism project and a migratory bird study, astrophysical observatories from Cambridge, Massachusetts, to Chile, and laboratories in the tropical forest of Panama. The Smithsonian's longstanding support of basic research has stimulated the development of many practical advances. Its funding of an unknown college professor named Robert Goddard in the early twentieth century led to the discovery of the principles of rocket propulsion and launched the space age; field research in the Yukon revealed vast natural resources in the years before Congress decided to acquire the Alaska Territory; and the Federal Bureau of Investigation's frequent calls on the Natural History Museum's expert anthropologists and their encyclopedic collections led to the founding of the field of forensic analysis. Through this work, the impact of Smithson's name on society has been immense.

But Henry was certainly mistaken about the dangers of architectural showpieces. The castellated Smithsonian building he opposed so vigorously has become the iconic symbol of the institution and an architectural landmark. It was joined in subsequent decades by numerous other significant buildings designed expressly for the Smithsonian by major architects, such as Charles A. Platt, Gordon Bunshaft, and Gyo Obata. In the breadth of all the Smithsonian buildings, including those acquired over time—among them one of the nation's finest Greek Revival public buildings—can be seen a microcosm of the history of American architecture. This book offers an introduction to the Smithsonian's architecture as it explores how the Smithsonian has grown over the course of its more than 160-year history, beginning with the Castle and carrying through to the National Museum of the American Indian.

When the Castle was completed in 1855, it became the first public building on the Mall. The famed Civil War photographer Mathew Brady's image shows it rising above the tree-lined Smithsonian Park. At the time the U.S. Capitol dome was still under construction.

Joseph Henry and his family lived for many years in the Castle's east wing. In 1862 they were photographed on the Smithsonian grounds near their home by the famous American artist Titian Ramsay Peale.

Reflecting the Arts and Industries Building's origins, its north entrance boasts the inscription National Museum, 1879. Patterns of multicolored brick, which decorate all sides of the red brick building, are clearly seen above the tall, arched windows.

The Smithsonian's founding act made it the national repository for the collections of the United States, and the development of its buildings is inextricably tied to the history and the growth of these collections. As government expeditions fanned out to chart and study the West, explorers sent back to Washington tens of thousands of specimens. The first Smithsonian building, the red sandstone Castle, rapidly filled with artifacts and specimens (and with the young men who studied and catalogued them, while living in the little rooms high in the Castle's towers). It housed the ethnographic and archeological collections, minerals and meteorites, dinosaurs, historic relics, botanical and natural history specimens, and paintings and sculpture.

The Philadelphia Centennial Exhibition of 1876, for which the Smithsonian was charged with preparing all the government's exhibits, celebrated the nation's emerging economic and industrial strength. The history of technology soon became one of the institution's more prominent fields of collecting. With the influx of material that came to Washington after the fair, the need for a new building became overwhelming. Congress responded, and the exuberant polychrome brick building now known as Arts and Industries was begun in 1879 and completed two years later. It was the first building dedicated entirely to the U.S. National Museum, cementing the Smithsonian's role as curator of the national collections. Over the course of the next half century, the institution was a significant presence at many expositions and world's fairs—which in turn ensured that the collections continued to expand exponentially.

Surrounded by their specimens, curators in ethnology at the turn of the twentieth century work on a newly installed Arts and Industries Building balcony—added to accommodate the burgeoning collections.

Within a few years of the completion of the Arts and Industries Building came the need for yet more space, in particular room for storage and curatorial work. The Smithsonian began to appeal to Congress as early as 1885, pleas that continued on a regular basis until construction started in 1903 on a new building for the National Museum (the Natural History Museum, across the Mall from the Castle). Separate facilities for research work began in the 1890s, with the construction of a utilitarian wooden shed for the Astrophysical Observatory in the South Yard behind the Castle.

The story of the growth of the Smithsonian and its collections is entwined with the development of the National Mall. Congress allocated the Smithsonian a fifty-acre plot, between Seventh and Twelfth Streets, as part of its original establishment. These grounds were landscaped in a romantic style by Andrew Jackson Downing (1815–52) in the early 1850s, with heavily wooded areas and curving carriage paths. As the Smithsonian expanded, its new museum buildings—

An 1882 plan for the grounds of the Smithsonian shows the park-like nature of the site before the McMillan Commission of 1901 reshaped the Mall as it appears today. The buildings shown are the long, narrow Castle, the square Arts and Industries Building, and the E-shaped Army Medical Museum. Adolf Cluss designed both the Arts and Industries Building and the Medical Museum. The tiny square to the left of the Castle was the Laboratory of Natural History, where taxidermists and the institution's photographer worked.

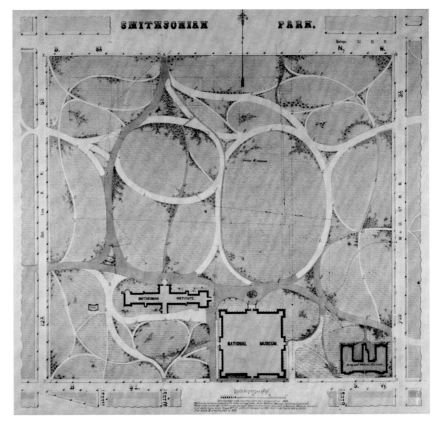

Arts and Industries, Natural History, and the Freer—were all built within the original bounds of this Smithsonian Park. During the second half of the nineteenth century, these grounds remained quite distinct from the rest of the area now known as the Mall, which included the Agriculture Department, with its botanical gardens; the Armory, with its supporting buildings; and even the Baltimore and Potomac train station, whose rail line cut across the Mall and its park areas.

When the McMillan Commission undertook to create a Beaux-Arts style for Washington in 1901, it focused on turning the Victorian Mall into a grand neoclassical greensward reminiscent of Pierre Charles L'Enfant's original vision for the capital. The Capitol and the Washington Monument were to be linked in one ensemble, creating an architectural stage set suited to the rising republic. The great open space of the newly designed Mall between these public monuments would, according to the commission, afford "spacious sites for buildings devoted to scientific purposes and to the great museums." The Smithsonian's Natural History Museum, with its imposing classical portico and Roman dome, became a model for the new classical architecture that was to define the city's monumental core. In its large-scale classical massing and its careful siting on the north side of the Mall, Natural History set a precedent for the museums that would follow.

The Natural History Museum launched the great neoclassical era for public buildings in the capital. Rising above its Corinthian columns is the low, Roman dome designed by Daniel Burnham and Charles Follen McKim.

The Small Mammal House, shown soon after its completion in 1906, is now the oldest building at the National Zoological Park. Known today as the Think Tank, it was designed by Hornblower and Marshall, the architects of the Natural History Museum.

The expansion of the Smithsonian at the outset of the twentieth century was driven in large part by the acquisition of new collections—items that resulted from the pursuit of different aspects of the original congressional charter. Although a "gallery of art" had been included in the 1846 act and existed in the Castle at the time of its completion in 1855, it was not really until the turn of the next century, under the third secretary, Samuel P. Langley (1834–1906), that the Smithsonian began to focus on collecting art. In 1906 Harriet Lane Johnston, the niece and White House hostess of President James Buchanan, donated a large number of paintings, which formed the nucleus of the original National Gallery of Art, founded under the Smithsonian's auspices. (Later it became the National Collection of Fine Arts and today is the Smithsonian American Art Museum.) This was followed by the donation of Charles Lang Freer's extraordinary collection of Asian art and the funds to build the Freer Gallery, the first Smithsonian museum dedicated exclusively to the fine arts. Freer's gift to the nation continued a tradition of philanthropy started by none other than Smithson himself; it was one carried on later in the century by Joseph Hirshhorn, with his modern art and sculpture collections and the ring-shaped building and garden to house it. This tradition of the self-made-man-turned-benefactor—one that became increasingly defined as American—is also an important element of the Smithsonian story and the development of its buildings.

The Smithsonian's architecture reflects the acquisition and the growth of the collections, but it also reveals a changing understanding of museology, of how to present items to the public, and of how to care for and curate them. This relationship is perhaps nowhere more evident than in the Smithsonian's National Zoological Park. The zoo's oldest extant building, the original Small Mammal House of 1906 (today called the Think Tank), is a typical nineteenth-century menagerie building; it stands in stark contrast to the barless moat design of the nearby Lion and Tiger House of the 1970s or the new Elephant Trails project designed to permit the animals to live and roam in a herd. In the case of the U.S. National Museum, the initial exhibits were accommodated within the linear plan of the Castle building. George Brown Goode, an early curator, did pioneering work in museum studies using the flexible square plan of the Arts and Industries Building as his laboratory. In terms of floor plan and exhibition display, the leap from the Castle to Arts and Industries was a large one, but the jump from the open-plan pavilions of Arts and Industries to the monumental halls of the Natural History Museum was even greater. Both the Castle and Arts and Industries "furnished many valuable object lessons," explained Smithsonian leaders at the completion of the new Natural History building, "teaching perhaps more what to avoid than what to retain, and in the prolonged effort to adapt them to the storage and exhibition of the constantly overflowing collections it was but natural that very definite opinions should have been reached as to the general and detailed requirements of a modern museum."

The idea of what constituted a modern museum had changed a great deal by the 1964 opening of the Museum of History and Technology, as the National Museum of American History was originally known. Likewise born of a reevaluation of the best means to display collections and educate and engage visitors, it was the culmination of a program of exhibition modernization that the Smithsonian undertook in the 1950s. Key leaders of this charge were Secretary Leonard Carmichael (1898–1973) and the curator who became the founding director of the Museum of History and Technology, Frank Taylor. The advances of that age—the replacement of glass-fronted cases with large built-out dioramas, which created contained environments but obscured a building's original features—are slowly being undone some forty years later; examples can be seen in the new Kenneth E. Behring Family Hall of Mammals and the Sant Ocean Hall in the Natural History Museum.

When completed in 1964, the American History Museum's recessed bays, lighted at night, subtly recalled the colonnaded Lincoln Memorial at the western end of the Mall. Its modern exterior was mirrored inside by innovative exhibition spaces.

Except for a single window on the Mall side, the design of the Hirshhorn Museum (left) restricted windows to the internal courtyard. Sculpture galleries in the museum encircle this protected space, which is enlivened by a central fountain.

The Smithsonian's Jupiter-C Missile exhibit (opposite, left) was installed in 1959 on what was known as Rocket Row, on the west side of the Arts and Industries Building. At the time there was nowhere else to display the institution's growing spacecraft collection.

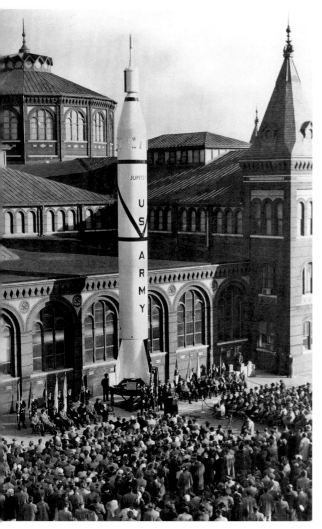

The vast interior galleries of the National Air and Space Museum, opened in 1976, easily accommodate missiles that once would have fit only outdoors on Rocket Row.

The modernization campaign at midcentury heralded a period of tremendous growth for the Smithsonian, especially in the arts. The National Museum of American History, when it opened in 1964, was the first new Smithsonian building on the Mall since the Freer in 1923. Despite its sleek modernity, it marked the continuation of the McMillan's Plan's vision of a National Mall lined with monumental, classically inspired museums. It was followed by the Hirshhorn and the National Air and Space Museum, further variations on a theme of modernism. From four buildings on the Mall for much of the first half of the twentieth century, the Smithsonian counted ten there as the twenty-first century dawned.

The Old Patent Office Building was adapted for use as the Smithsonian American Art Museum and the National Portrait Gallery. Past the original Model Hall (above), now the Luce Foundation Center, glass panels today provide a glimpse of open art storage and conservators at work in the Lunder Conservation Center.

Modern art has been exhibited in the American Art Museum's Lincoln Gallery since 1968. Abraham Lincoln had his second inaugural ball in this columned space.

During the 1960s and 1970s, the Smithsonian became a leader in the adaptation and reuse of historic buildings. Of the new museums to join the Smithsonian collection then, many of them were housed in historic structures. The National Collection of Fine Arts (now the Smithsonian American Art Museum) and the National Portrait Gallery opened in the Old Patent Office Building, one of the most important buildings of early Washington. The Renwick Gallery of Art, dedicated to American crafts and decorative arts, brought life back to the original Corcoran Gallery of Art, an exquisite example of the French Second Empire style, designed by James Renwick Jr., the talented architect of the original Smithsonian Castle. The Cooper-Hewitt National Design Museum took over Andrew Carnegie's mansion in New York City, preserving both building and collection. The Old Patent Office Building and the Renwick had each been used for decades as offices; reuse ensured their restoration as well as public access.

During the Civil War, the museum building that became the Renwick Gallery of Art served as offices for the quartermaster general, Montgomery C. Meigs. The 1824 house to the right is now part of Blair House, the presidential guest complex.

This period of expansion at the Smithsonian mirrored a time of social upheaval in the United States, an era when the civil rights and women's movements were bringing new perspectives to the telling and exploration of American history. To reach new constituencies, the Smithsonian opened the Anacostia Neighborhood Museum in 1967. It was an experiment to take the Smithsonian off the Mall—in the words of Secretary S. Dillon Ripley (1913–2001), to make it a less forbidding collection of marble halls. The Smithsonian's growth at this time also acquired an increasingly global outlook, as the institution saw itself in dialogue with the larger world, Africa and Asia in particular. The Folklife Festival, celebrating living cultural heritage traditions from around the world, was inaugurated on the Mall in 1967. As part of a Festival of India, the Natural History Museum hosted Aditi: The Living Arts of India in 1985, and in 1986 a major Russian art show, with rarely loaned works from the Soviet Union, came to the Renwick Gallery. The Smithsonian worked with Ghana in the early 1990s to establish a museum in the Cape Coast Castle, a seventeenth-century coastal fortress used in the trans-Atlantic slave trade.

A variety of African sources inspired the architecture of the Anacostia Community Museum. Red brick walls evoke woven Kente cloth, while cylinders with diamonds of glass block and blue tile recall eleventh-century towers of Great Zimbabwe.

Charles Lindbergh flies the Spirit of St. Louis over Gatun Lake in the Panama Canal Zone in 1928. The first home of the Smithsonian's Tropical Research Institute was on Barro Colorado Island, in the middle of the lake. Lindbergh's plane now resides at the Air and Space Museum.

The first research laboratory of the Tropical Research Institute was on top of Barro Colorado Island. Small tracks at the left brought supplies to the scientists in 1950. Today the wooden building serves as the visitors center.

Proximity to three of the Smithsonian's historic structures—the Castle, the Arts and Industries Building, and the Freer Gallery (not visible here)—made underground construction of the Quadrangle challenging (above).

The round domes of the African Art Museum's entrance pavilion (opposite), which contrast with the pyramidal roofs of the Sackler Gallery, were inspired in part by African architectural forms as well as by the round arches of the Freer Gallery across the Quadrangle.

This global outlook led ultimately to the creation of the Quadrangle in 1987, which encompasses the Arthur M. Sackler Gallery, the National Museum of African Art, the S. Dillon Ripley International Center, and the Enid A. Haupt Garden. It was "time to look beyond our immediate horizon," said Ripley, who considered the Quadrangle one of the most significant projects the Smithsonian had ever undertaken. The Quadrangle was also a clever rethinking of the South Yard behind the Castle, which had spawned so many Smithsonian initiatives—from the taxidermy sheds where exhibit preparation for the world's fairs took place, to the animal enclosures that led to the National Zoo, to the observatory shed that formed the embryonic Astrophysical Observatory, to the Quonset hut that housed the first National Air Museum. This area, once dedicated to behind-the-scenes work, is now a public showcase. With the creation of the pioneering Museum Support Center in Suitland, Maryland, in 1983, storage, research, and conservation spaces acquired their own dedicated building complex.

The more recent growth of the Smithsonian has focused on broadening the narrative and understanding of the American experience and displaying it in all its diversity. In 1997 the Smithsonian Latino Center was created to celebrate Latino heritage and culture, and the Asian Pacific American Program was established the following year. The National Museum of the American Indian was developed as a living museum, its design and presentation created in consultation with numerous

tribes across North and South America. The National Museum of African American History and Culture, established in 2003, has commenced the design process for its building site to the west of the National Museum of American History. Dedicated to exploring African American culture, it has opened its doors already with an extensive and interactive virtual presence on the Web.

More than a century and a half after the establishment of the Smithsonian, the institution comprises—perhaps to what would be Joseph Henry's chagrin—an extraordinary collection of bricks and mortar. Six of the buildings in which Smithsonian museums are located are National Historic Landmarks, the country's highest preservation designation and one that connotes exceptional national significance. Even the Smithsonian's fondly bestowed nickname, the "Nation's Attic," denotes a type of architectural space: a great national place, stuffed to the gills with all of those things we wish to remember, the cultural and scientific heritage that seems best to define the United States. These buildings that serve as repositories of the nation's history are themselves a rich and important collection, representative of the scope of American architectural history and an essential part of the Smithsonian.

THE CASTLE

The turreted red sandstone Castle building, a landmark of American architecture, has been the symbol of the Smithsonian for more than 150 years. Before it was built, Washington, D.C., was a city of monumental neoclassical buildings: the White House, the Capitol, the Treasury Building, and the Old Patent Office Building (which today houses the Smithsonian American Art Museum and the National Portrait Gallery). The arrival of the Smithsonian's first building, with its nine dark asymmetrical towers and its fortresslike embattlements, represented a powerful departure from this classicism and marked the introduction of picturesque styles in American public architecture.

The choice of a medieval revival style for the Smithsonian building was deliberate. Although the classical models that dominated Washington's public buildings evoked ancient Greece and Rome, the Castle's Romanesque form allied the building symbolically with historic English collegiate architecture, like that of Oxford and Cambridge. It visually captured the unique mix of public function and private monies, as well as the English origin, represented by James Smithson's bequest. This distinction was expressed as well in the choice of building material. The red sandstone, quarried in Seneca, Maryland, and brought to the site on the Chesapeake and Ohio Canal, stood in striking contrast to the pale Aquia Creek sandstone used for the capital's earlier public buildings.

This 1860 engraving is one of the few known images of James Renwick Jr., architect of the Castle. He also designed the building that became the Renwick Gallery of Art.

The architect was James Renwick Jr. (1818–95), a talented and well-connected twenty-eight-year-old New Yorker, who won the 1846 competition held by the building committee of the newly chartered Smithsonian. Renwick was the son of an amateur architect and already much admired for his Gothic Revival Grace Church in New York City, which he had designed in 1843. The style of the Smithsonian building was intended from the beginning as a model for the nation. Even before it was completed, the design was discussed in an 1849 book, *Hints on Public Architecture*, in which Robert Dale Owen (1801–77), a regent who was the building committee chairman, made the case for a new, picturesque national style of architecture for America.

The building had to house many activities. When Congress passed the 1846 act establishing the Smithsonian Institution, it called for the creation of a museum, laboratories, a library, lecture halls, a gallery of art, and more. Believing that the institution's success depended on a building that could "make conspicuous the work of the organization," Owen advocated a large, showy structure. The accommodation of the multifaceted original functions is still readable on the Castle's exterior.

The Romanesque-style Smithsonian building (above) was first presented to the public in Hints on Public Architecture. The 1849 book by Robert Dale Owen, a regent of the institution, argued that picturesque revival styles should be the basis for a new national architecture.

The cover page of Owen's Hints on Public Architecture (right) introduced readers to the medieval revival style, exemplified by Renwick's design for the Smithsonian.

As depicted in Hints on Public Architecture, the chapel-like west end of the Castle (left) originally had an open loggia that provided a walkway.

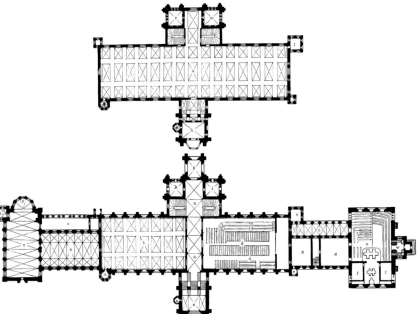

The noted photographer
Andrew J. Russell captured the
Smithsonian Castle (above)
about 1858, when the Mall was
planted in a romantic style
that included wildflowers.

James Renwick's floor plan of the
Smithsonian's first building (left),
published in Hints on Public
Architecture, shows the earliest
configuration of the Castle.

The North Tower (opposite) is
the tallest of the Castle's nine
towers. It now houses a bell, cast
at the Whitechapel Foundry in
London for the Smithsonian's
150th anniversary in 1996, that
rings every hour.

In 1849 the stout eastern end of the building, with its heavy crenellation and contrastingly delicate chimney-pot piers, became the first part to be completed. For more than a year, all of the work of the Smithsonian was carried out within its walls. Once the entire building was finished in 1855, this original section provided office and laboratory space and the important International Exchange Service, which disseminated scientific publications around the world. For twenty-three years it also contained living quarters for the Smithsonian's first secretary, Joseph Henry, and his family. In the Smithsonian's first decades, others lived in the building as well, including a number of young naturalists who had bedrooms high up in the towers. The east wing of the building underwent a major reconstruction in the early 1880s, after Joseph Henry's death. New floors of office space were inserted in fireproof materials by Adolf Cluss and Paul Schulze, the architects of the Smithsonian's second building, the Arts and Industries Building.

The Castle's west wing resembles a chapel. It even had a cloister along the north facade of the connecting range (which is now enclosed and forms part of Schermer Hall). Beautifully lighted, with skylights and a rose window as well as clerestory windows, the west wing was intended originally as one of the building's lecture halls; the apselike end would have provided an excellent speaker's platform. It was also ideal for a gallery of art and later served as exhibition space, but when the building first opened this area contained the Smithsonian's library.

The Castle's South Yard (opposite) contains the Enid A. Haupt Garden. Nineteenth-century garden furniture, reflective of the building's Victorian origins, are scattered throughout the grounds.

A fanlight tympanum over the South Tower door (bottom left), which leads into the space that once contained the Children's Room, was carved from Seneca sandstone in 1984 according to Renwick's original design.

A statue of St. Dunstan (bottom right), patron saint of blacksmiths, was given to the Smithsonian in 1980 by Westminster Abbey. It is in an elevated niche on the east side of the South Tower that Renwick intended for a sculpture.

The Star-Spangled Banner hangs at the Castle's east end in 1914, soon after its arrival at the Smithsonian. The flag was painstakingly restored in the west end of the building by a team of seamstresses.

Visitors view the natural history collections in the Castle's two-hundred-foot-long Great Hall (opposite) two years after the 1865 fire. Balconies encircled the space, which was dominated by two rows of piers decorated with clustered columns and ornate capitals.

The central block, with its giant two-story rounded windows, accommodated the museum galleries and other public functions. By placing the staircases in the towers, the main floors could be left open. The grand, central space on the ground floor, called the Great Hall, was originally some two hundred feet long; it is dominated by two rows of immense arched piers, each consisting of clusters of slender columns culminating in delicate, ornate capitals. The upper story, in its first iteration, housed a lecture hall that could accommodate 1,500 persons, an art gallery, and an apparatus room where scientific experiments were demonstrated. In 1865 the upper portion of the building was destroyed in a fire. When it was rebuilt, using fireproof materials, the space was put to new use. It became a museum gallery, housing many of the items that would form the core of the Natural History Museum collections.

The Children's Room (above) opened in 1901 with the theme Knowledge Begins in Wonder. Hands-on exhibits and low-level cases were installed to engage young visitors. This 1920 view is one of the last depictions of the room before it was altered for office space. The original paint colors and decorative ceiling have since been restored.

Bison—then in danger of extinction in the West—grazed in the South Yard behind the Castle (right) in the late 1880s, before the National Zoological Park was established in 1889.

The Smithsonian quickly became the natural repository for the government's scientific collections. In 1858 all of the items that had been on display at the Patent Office, many of them from the U.S. Exploring Expedition of 1838–42, came to the Castle. As America continued to explore the West, more and more specimens were shipped back to Washington. Soon the burgeoning collections threatened to overwhelm the Smithsonian building. The responsibilities that came with curating these objects drove the first secretary to seek an appropriation from Congress in 1858 for their care; this marked the beginning within the Smithsonian of the U.S. National Museum, which received funding for its own structure (the Arts and Industries Building) in 1879.

Most of the Smithsonian's later museums and many of its research programs had their start in or around the Castle. A pioneering Children's Room was created in the South Tower in 1901, with a decorative scheme by the designer Grace Lincoln Temple; its cases were at children's eye level and the objects had labels in English rather than Latin. Other Smithsonian initiatives—such as the Radiation Biology Laboratory, the graphic arts collections, and the ethnology, archeology, and anthropology collections—had their beginnings in the Castle. Even the National Zoological Park emerged from the South Yard behind the building, where bison threatened with extinction in the West were kept for several years in the late 1880s. The Smithsonian is also one of very few museums in the world to hold the tomb of its founder. James Smithson's remains, housed today in a crypt that features Smithson's original Italian sarcophagus, were brought from Italy in the early twentieth century by Alexander Graham Bell.

As the Smithsonian expanded and new museum buildings were constructed, the role of the Castle changed. In the 1960s the building became host to a center for scholars, with the upper hall divided into two floors to accommodate the new Woodrow Wilson International Center for Scholars (now located nearby in the Ronald Reagan Building and International Trade Center). Today the Castle, a National Historic Landmark, functions as the institution's administrative heart and contains the offices of top Smithsonian officials. It is furnished with Victorian furniture and decorative arts from the Castle Collection, one of the country's few collections of historic furniture to be actively used. Since 1972 a welcome center has been housed in the Great Hall, providing an orientation to the many museums that grew out of this building, the first home of the National Museum.

Elizabeth II visits James Smithson's crypt at the Castle's north entrance during the U.S. Bicentennial in 1976. Behind her are Chief Justice Warren Burger, head of the Board of Regents, and Secretary S. Dillon Ripley.

The Arts and Industries Building, which opened in 1881, was the first structure specifically designed to house the U.S. National Museum. With its exuberant Victorian polychrome work, the building stands today as one of the finest examples of nineteenth-century exposition architecture in the nation. Built quickly and inexpensively of fireproof masonry construction, it was groundbreaking for its time in size, floor plan, and use of technology. Throughout much of its history, the building served as an incubator for the latest in exhibition design. In fact, four future Smithsonian museums—Natural History, American History, American Art, and Air and Space—emerged from collections originally displayed in this building.

Ornament throughout the Arts and Industries Building, such as this exterior gate with a floral medallion, followed the ideals of nineteenth-century reformers who called for designs derived from nature.

The need for a new museum arose directly from the overcrowding of the original Smithsonian building. The space problem in the Castle had become dire by the 1870s, when the Smithsonian began amassing new material to display at the Philadelphia Centennial Exhibition of 1876. Exhibits there focused on the institution's work and featured "a display of the mineral and animal resources, as well as of the ethnology, of the United States." At the conclusion of the fair, all of these objects, together with those of many federal agencies and a number of exhibits presented by foreign governments, made their way by the trainload to the Smithsonian. The overload caused Spencer F. Baird (1823–87), the head of the museum and the man who would become the institution's second secretary, to declare a state of emergency. Appeals were made to Congress, which authorized funding for a new building in 1879.

The architects selected by the building committee for the new museum, Adolf Cluss (1825–1905) and Paul Schulze (1827–97), had come to the United States from Germany in 1848, the year of the European revolutions. Cluss had been active in radical circles and corresponded with Karl Marx for several years, even after the architect had moved to the United States. Notwithstanding his early political ties, he thrived in the American capital, founded the local Republican Party, and was a prominent Washington, D.C., citizen. From 1862 to 1876, he designed or oversaw all of the public buildings erected by the District of Columbia government. Cluss's reputation as an outstanding engineer-architect was an important factor in his selection by the Smithsonian. He was later instrumental in renovations at the Castle and the Old Patent Office Building after major fires.

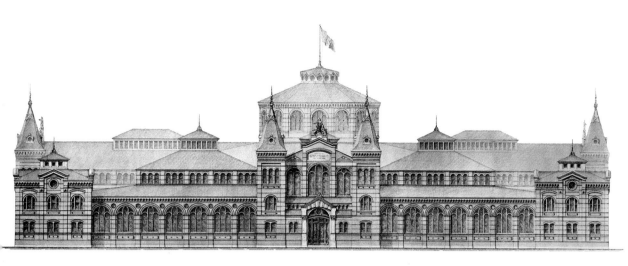

Cluss and Schulze's design for the National Museum, which echoed the pavilion-style buildings popular at the 1876 Philadelphia fair, focused on providing maximum floor space for exhibitions. Some 328 feet square, it was divided into four quadrants, using an equilateral floor plan that took its inspiration from writings on ideal museums by the French theorist J. N. L. Durand. The building's external design was generated by this plan, with each entrance flanked by symmetrical towers and incorporating a tiled, covered vestibule to protect visitors from inclement weather.

Cluss and Schulze's 1879 elevation drawing shows the colorful brickwork and the many large, round-arch windows then considered ideal lighting for museum exhibition space.

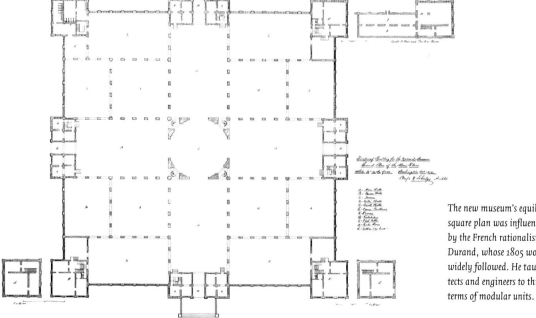

The new museum's equilateral square plan was influenced by the French rationalist J. N. L. Durand, whose 1805 work was widely followed. He taught architects and engineers to think in terms of modular units.

The rapid construction of the new National Museum building (above) was documented by the Smithsonian photographer Thomas W. Smillie from the roof of the Castle.

The building committee for the National Museum stands in an unfinished doorway of the new building (right). From left to right are General Montgomery C. Meigs; General William Tecumseh Sherman, building committee chairman; Peter Parker, a regent; Spencer F. Baird, Smithsonian secretary; Adolf Cluss, architect; W. J. Rhees, chief clerk; and Daniel Leech, correspondence clerk.

The interior layout was unprecedented in its use of an open-wall interpretation of the Durand plan. Seventeen halls were organized around a central rotunda, with four main double-height halls extending in cardinal directions. Openings in the masonry walls permitted light to pour in from skylights and clerestory windows above and then filter through every public space in the building. Cluss and Schulze, respectful of the Romanesque style of the original Smithsonian building, used rounded arches throughout the interior and the exterior to complement the Castle. The walls were ornamented with stenciled decorative borders and panels, in colors derived from nature—from bright yellow sunlight to deep lavender shadows.

The building was so spectacular that even before it officially opened to the public, it hosted President James A. Garfield's inaugural ball in March 1881. While in Congress, Garfield had served as a regent of the Smithsonian. More than five thousand guests attended, many arriving in carriages. The building was illuminated, giving the event an air of modern fantasy, and the interior was filled with flowers, tropical plants, sculpture, flags, and draped bunting. Gas lighting was temporarily installed inside for the event, which prompted the city's *Evening Star* to report that the ball was "the largest and most brilliantly held . . . the new museum building was conspicuous from a long distance, its lights within giving a good view of its outlines and making it resemble a crystal palace."

The new museum building contained one of the city's largest indoor spaces. It was splendidly decorated by Adolf Cluss for James A. Garfield's inaugural ball on March 4, 1881.

With its polychrome brick, slate-covered turrets, and arched windows of Belgian glass, the exterior's whimsical appearance disguises the fact that the building—under thirty-seven separate roof structures—was one of the most technologically innovative of its time. Exposed on the interior, the roof support system was made of wrought-iron trusses; this new technology, developed following the Civil War, was stronger and lighter than cast iron and not prone to rust. At the ridge line, the roof also supported lanterns (long galleried windows) that could ventilate the interior as hot air rose. The enormous operable windows of the main exhibition spaces provided both light and ventilation. Hot water heating, gas and electric lighting, telegraph lines, telephones, sewer connections, and even burglar alarms were all part of this state-of-the-art building when it opened. Bricks, in red and buff, were fabricated with a new hydraulic pressed-brick method. Their use reflected the latest architectural theories: strong horizontal bands of black-colored bricks signaled structural elements, such as towers, buttresses, and pavilions; bricks with smooth, glazed color finishes created a yellow and blue basket-weave pattern to indicate the decorative and non-load-bearing curtain walls. Corbelling (stepping) of bricks provided a pleasing texture at the cornice line, while terra-cotta medallions set between arched windows in the ranges featured plant-inspired designs.

The simple appearance of the roof above the interior rotunda hides a sophisticated design (above). Rigid supports in alternating straight and angled positions produce a hypnotic pattern.

A cast-zinc sculptural group, Columbia Protecting Arts and Industry (left), by Caspar Buberl, rises over the Mall entrance. Representing the nation, Columbia wears a headdress of five-point stars. The figure Arts is reading a book with an owl, representing knowledge, while Industry holds the tools of the nineteenth century's new industries.

Visitors flocked to the new museum at the turn of century (opposite). The formal limestone-framed entrance is one of four into the building.

Before construction of the balcony galleries in 1897–1902, interiors were open and spacious. There was no need for lighting fixtures, as natural light streamed through the open windows and skylights.

Offices were located in the corner pavilions, anchoring the exhibition halls. Here three men share a typical Smithsonian office of the nineteenth century, replete with gas lighting, glass-fronted bookcases, and a spittoon in the foreground.

Within a few years, however, the building was overflowing with collections, a problem that persisted even after balconies were inserted in the four corner courts in 1897–1902 by the local architects Hornblower and Marshall. These mezzanine spaces, with Beaux-Arts–detailed iron railings as well as stairs connecting to the rotunda, increased space for a while, but as the collections grew even larger, staff continued to complain of the lack of storage and work space. After nearly twenty years of appeals for a new building, Congress appropriated $3.5 million in 1903. When the new National Museum of Natural History was completed across the Mall in 1911, it was dedicated to the collections of natural and human history. The Smithsonian's nascent gallery of art was also transferred to the new museum. Cluss and Schulze's innovative structure retained the collections emphasizing the industrial arts, technology, and American history, and it was renamed the Arts and Industries Building.

Its collections, which became the core of the future National Museum of History and Technology (today the National Museum of American History), also eventually outgrew the building. When the Smithsonian embarked on an exhibition modernization program in the 1950s and 1960s, many ideas were tested first at the Arts and Industries Building. The Museum of History and Technology, completed in 1964, became the showpiece of the Smithsonian's newest presentation ideas. Arts and Industries was then transformed into a site for temporary exhibitions, but it continued to be dominated by growing air and space collections. Planes such as the Wright Brothers' 1903 Flyer and Lindbergh's *Spirit of St. Louis* hung overhead in the galleries, and the group of rockets forming Rocket Row rose high over the building's west side. The opening of the National Air and Space Museum in 1976 freed up the building once more.

Arts and Industries underwent an extensive rehabilitation in the 1970s under the direction of the noted local architect Hugh Newell Jacobsen (b. 1929). The four two-story internal courts were filled in to provide additional office and work space, and the building systems and roof were upgraded. In this newly restored space, a popular exhibition recreating the 1876 Philadelphia Centennial Exhibition opened in time for the U.S. Bicentennial celebrations in 1976. The exhibition and the building were so well suited that visitors could literally step back in time.

Beginning in 1914, the First Ladies' gowns (seen here in 1931) became the Smithsonian's most popular exhibit. In an early conservation effort, fabric covered the windows to filter light.

In recent years the Arts and Industries Building, a National Historic Landmark, has housed a variety of temporary art, history, and horticulture exhibitions, as well as the popular Discovery Theatre. In 2004, however, the building was closed to the public because of structural deterioration. Plans are now under way for the building's rehabilitation and reuse.

The museum's open-arch walls provide clear sight lines through the building. Charles Lindbergh's Spirit of St. Louis was suspended from the roof trusses shortly after his historic 1927 flight across the Atlantic.

NATIONAL ZOOLOGICAL PARK

At the time of its founding in 1889, the National Zoological Park was unlike any other zoo in the world. Most nineteenth-century zoos, such as ones in Philadelphia and Cincinnati, were small urban menageries designed primarily for the entertainment of visitors. The National Zoo was the first zoo planned as a breeding park and a wildlife refuge for the preservation of North American species. It encompassed approximately 170 acres in Rock Creek Park, on what was then the outskirts of Washington, D.C.

The zoo was the inspiration of the Smithsonian's taxidermist, William Temple Hornaday (1854–1937). On a collecting trip to Montana in the late 1880s, he was shocked at the decimation of the American bison, which he called "the most striking and conspicuous species on this continent." Hornaday enlisted the Smithsonian to help secure the animal's preservation and published *The Extermination of the American Bison*. While Congress debated a proposal to establish a zoological park, the seeds of the National Zoo began with the collection of live bison Hornaday maintained behind the Castle (see page 38). Believing that the zoo would principally benefit local residents—rather than serving as a national endeavor—Congress initially created it in conjunction with the District of Columbia and specified that half of its budget come from the city.

Secretary Samuel P. Langley (at center, facing out) talks with William Temple Hornaday in 1888, surrounded by a party of men surveying the Rock Creek property that would soon become the National Zoo. The zoo's landscape architect, Frederick Law Olmsted, is the figure in light clothing and a bowler hat.

The physical plan for the zoo was conceived by the famed landscape architect Frederick Law Olmsted (1822–1903), the designer of Central Park in New York City. It featured a long, broad, winding path (today called Olmsted Walk), with the main buildings clustered together at the center of the property. Olmsted's fellow Massachusetts architect William Ralph Emerson designed a number of the early animal houses, such as the Buffalo Barn and the first Lion House (known variously at first as the Carnivora House). These picturesque buildings, made of rustic, local stone or wood, capitalized on the natural features of Rock Creek Park and were meant to evoke ideas of the American wilderness.

William Ralph Emerson's
Buffalo House of 1891 (above)
evoked the rustic log cabins
of the American frontier. It was
demolished in the 1930s.

Ten wooden cages, known as
"Rotten Row," encircle the
Raccoon House in 1935 (left).
Some of these cages were moved
from the Castle's South Yard to
the zoo when it opened.

The National Zoo experienced a heyday in the first half of the twentieth century under William Mann (1886–1960), a gregarious and enterprising leader who served as director for more than twenty-five years. He (and often his wife, Lucile Quarry Mann) traveled around the world on expeditions, such as the Smithsonian-Chrysler Expedition to East Africa in 1926, the National Geographic-Smithsonian Expedition to the Dutch East Indies in 1937, and the Firestone-Smithsonian Expedition to Liberia in 1940, bringing thousands of new animals to the zoo. Many of the major animal houses were built during these years, including the Reptile House, the Bird House, the Elephant House, and the Small Mammal House. These buildings, designed by the municipal architect of Washington (first Albert Harris, and then Edward Clarke), were full of whimsy and architectural decoration, underscoring the emphasis on popular entertainment that flourished in these years. The structures incorporated animal imagery and sculpture inside and out, often in new, unusual materials, such as aluminum and colored concrete. Many of the pieces were created during the Great Depression by artists with the federal Works Progress Administration.

The fantastical Reptile House by Albert Harris was completed in 1931 in a Byzanto-Romanesque architectural style. It is covered with reptilian imagery, from turtles that hold up the columns of the main entrance porch to lizards and frogs that cling to the capitals.

Showing a typical early zoo interior of the 1900s, the bird house (left) was lighted in part by a skylight and doors with a large interior transom.

A Nubian giraffe and her baby, Bedella, stand in their Elephant House home (opposite) in 1949.

Masai giraffe occupy an enclosure in the Elephant House in 1938 (bottom). The mural was painted by artists from the Treasury Art Relief Project to give a sense of the animals' native habitat, one of many such decorative projects at the zoo in the 1930s and 1940s.

By the late 1950s the zoo's physical plant was deteriorating. A fatal accident at
the Lion House in 1958 forced the closure of six buildings and led to the creation
of the Friends of the National Zoo. FONZ's first achievement was to persuade
Congress to fund the zoo's entire budget, which eliminated the prior reliance on
District of Columbia government appropriations and enabled the Smithsonian
to embark on a period of renovation and renewal in Rock Creek. The zoo undertook a master plan in 1961 and then, from 1972 to 1990, an extensive new plan
created by Faulkner, Fryer and Vanderpool. The buildings of the latter period—
among them the Lion and Tiger House, the Great Ape House, and the administration building at the Connecticut Avenue entrance—were all concrete earth-
works set into the land. They embodied the period's growing environmental
awareness and emphasis on conservation. The popular giant pandas that are
such a symbol of the zoo today first arrived from China in 1972, following President Richard M. Nixon's historic visit; their addition to the zoo reflected its commitment to the study and preservation of endangered species and their habitats.

In the 1970s the National Zoo also acquired a large property in the Shenandoah
Valley near Front Royal, Virginia, for its Conservation and Research Center.
This 3,200-acre preserve, an army facility erected in 1912–16 to train cavalry
horses, is dedicated to conservation biology research and training. It propagates
rare species, including the black-footed ferret (the most endangered mammal
in the United States).

The zoo introduced the idea of a BioPark in the late 1980s, emphasizing exhibits that displayed entire ecosystems to visitors. These installations show plants and animals living together in their native environments, rather than relegating plants to a decorative or supporting role. Amazonia (1992)—at 15,000-square feet the largest and most complex exhibit at the zoo—reflects this new approach. It is a rainforest habitat featuring more than 350 plant species and dozens of species of mammals, birds, reptiles, amphibians, and insects native to the Amazon basin.

The National Zoological Park has embarked on a new master plan. The visitor facilities and animal habitats are being upgraded to reflect contemporary advances in knowledge of animal health and well-being. The plan also calls for the continued protection of the zoo's historic properties and the Rock Creek ecosystem. The Asia Trail, which debuted in 2006, leads visitors through a series of habitats and encounters with seven species, such as sloth bears, red pandas, and Asian small-clawed otters. It includes the Fujifilm Giant Panda Habitat, which mimics China's rocky, lush landscape and features grottoes and streams, bamboo stands and weeping willows, as well as a state-of-the-art research facility. Elephant Trails, an essential component of the zoo's Asian elephant conservation program, is a reconfiguration of the old Elephant House and surrounding areas intended to enable the animals to live as a herd and range more freely over a larger area. In keeping with the aims of the zoo, these new exhibits are closely entwined with the institution's research and conservation efforts.

The Lion and Tiger House (bottom left) by Faulkner, Fryer and Vanderpool was built in 1976. To respect the surrounding landscape, this and other concrete earthwork structures at the zoo were sunk into the earth to hide much of the actual structure.

Amazonia (1992, Cooper-Lecky), is the largest building at the zoo today (bottom right). A showcase of the BioPark concept, it presents the ecosystem of a tropical rainforest, together with animals that live in it.

NATIONAL MUSEUM OF NATURAL HISTORY

The National Museum of Natural History, which opened to the public in 1910 (a year before its completion), was the first building constructed on the Mall to reflect the ideals of the 1901 McMillan Commission. Intended to revive the eighteenth-century proposals of Pierre Charles L'Enfant for the federal city of Washington, the McMillan Plan reinstated the goal of monumental classicism and brought with it a sober Roman style. It transformed the Mall from a romantic, forested landscape with curving carriageways to the sweeping, open, formal greensward so familiar today, stretching from the Capitol to the Washington Monument. In its siting and its style, the Natural History Museum served as a prototype for a Beaux-Arts Washington.

The Washington, D.C., firm Hornblower and Marshall was selected to design the museum. At the time, it served as house architect for the Smithsonian, designing everything from Smithson's crypt (see page 39) and the Children's Room in the Castle (see page 38) to buildings at the zoo. To prepare for this monumental new building—intended also to embody the latest ideas for museum display, research laboratories, and public spaces—the architects made a tour of European museums. They studied all aspects of design, especially space allotment, exhibition cases, and lighting, noting exemplary placements of windows and skylights.

At the same time the head curators, notably William Henry Holmes, curator of prehistoric archeology, searched for model buildings. They canvassed museums around the world, asking for photographs, floor plans, guidebooks, and drawings. Holmes greatly influenced the successful plan for the Natural History Museum, particularly by calling for a large lecture hall. The building, as one Smithsonian official noted, marked "the beginning of a new year in the history of the National Museum, through the unrivaled conditions presented for the arrangement, care and safety of the collections." Richard Rathburn, a geologist who came to the institution in 1881, was appointed an assistant secretary in 1901; he oversaw the design and construction of the new building from 1901 until its completion.

William Henry Holmes (right), an archeologist, was the curator and first director of the Smithsonian's National Gallery of Art, which was housed in the Natural History Museum until it moved to the Old Patent Office Building in the 1960s. He is shown with fellow surviving members of the Hayden Survey of 1871–77, which explored the American West.

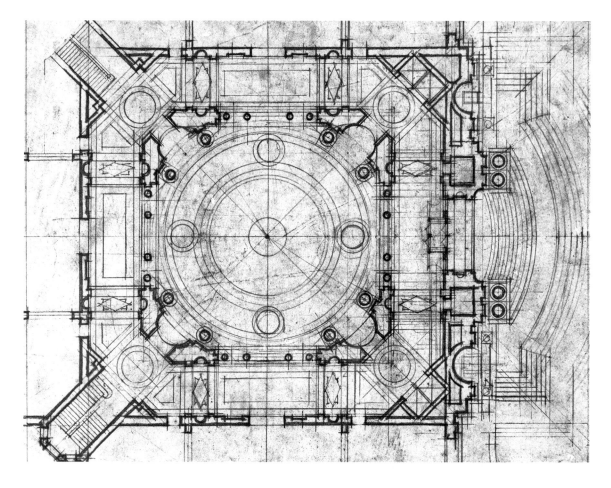

In 1905 the Smithsonian, unhappy with the ornate design of the planned dome, halted construction. Hornblower and Marshall experimented with ever-bolder articulations of the central pavilion and increased the dome's height, but Secretary Samuel P. Langley continued to withhold his approval. The impasse continued for a year, until it was broken by the design intervention of Daniel Burnham (1846–1912) and Charles Follen McKim (1847–1909) of McKim, Mead and White. McKim and Burnham were key members of the McMillan Commission, and Burnham was also the architect of one of its showpieces, Union Station, and the adjacent main post office (today the Smithsonian's National Postal Museum). McKim and Burnham substituted a sober, low Roman dome, tiled and placed on an attic story with semicircular windows based on those at the Baths of Diocletian. They also designed the massive columned portico facing the Mall, making the revised design a model for the classical buildings the McMillan Commission envisioned for Washington's monumental core.

Hornblower and Marshall's original drawing shows the formal floor plan of the three-story domed rotunda, from which all parts of the building radiate.

The fish-scale-tile dome of the Natural History Museum stands out from other local landmarks, including the FBI Building in the foreground and Reagan National Airport and the Masonic Temple in the distance at right.

The Smithsonian was thrilled with the dignified tone set by the new concept and immediately restarted construction. When the museum was completed in 1911, it was one of the largest public buildings in Washington (at more than one million square feet), second only to the Capitol. Hailed by the *Washington Post* as "the most remarkable structure of its kind in the world," it proved immensely popular and became the first Smithsonian museum to offer Sunday hours to accommodate the large number of visitors.

As befits the first Smithsonian museum of the twentieth century, this building is supported on a steel frame and includes two-story-high steel windows with decorative rosettes on the mullions. In contrast to the classical severity of the exterior, faced in granite, the interior central pavilion contains a dramatic, three-story octagonal domed rotunda. The subtle dome was constructed in the thin-shell technique devised by the Catalan architect Rafael Guastavino (1842–1908). On the level beneath the rotunda is the auditorium, an elegant circular room also sporting a Guastavino-tile dome. The great space of the rotunda has been dominated since 1959 by an enormous African bush elephant, which at the time of its unveiling was the largest land mammal on display in a museum. From this spot the building expands in three directions—south, west, and east—with grand, three-story-high halls lighted by skylights. This T-shaped plan originally incorporated two courtyards, providing light and air to the offices and laboratories encircling them. For a quarter century the building's coal furnaces supplied heat and hot water to the other Smithsonian buildings, using steam tunnels under the Mall.

J. J. Fenykovi, a big-game hunter, donated a two-ton elephant hide to the Smithsonian in 1953. Unveiled six years later, the Fenykovi elephant remains the centerpiece of the museum's rotunda. Balconies with decorative railings provide panoramic views of the grand space.

The museum's north side (above, seen in 1909) looked out onto the Center Market on B Street North. The street was renamed Constitution Avenue in 1931, when the market was demolished.

The museum was closed to the public from 1917 to 1919 for wartime activities. Hundreds of desks filled the exhibition space, where employees of the Bureau of War Risk Insurance worked (right).

The increasing breadth of the collections documenting the study of humans, plants, animals, and prehistory meant that yet again it was not long before additional space was required. In 1930 Congress authorized the construction of wings, but they were not funded until 1960. Designed by Mills, Petticourt and Mills, the six-story wings that were erected in the early 1960s were dedicated entirely to collections and staff laboratories. Their form, a modest modern interpretation of the original building, was shaped by two review standards: one, that additions to historic buildings avoid exactly copying the original design, and two, that the wings be set back from the main facade. With the expansion provided by this new space, the museum grew to eventually occupy just under two million square feet.

An aerial view of the museum in the early 1960s, before construction of the west wing, shows the new east wing at the right. The two original courtyards were filled in during the 1990s for an IMAX theater and visitor amenities on the west side and offices on the east.

The Hall of Extinct Monsters, now known as the Dinosaur Hall, includes the mural painting Diana of the Tides (1908), by John Eliot, in the background.

As the Smithsonian embarked on an institution-wide campaign of exhibition modernization in the 1950s and 1960s, many of the Natural History Museum halls were altered through renovations. Air conditioning and fluorescent lighting installed when the wings were constructed eliminated the need for natural light and open windows. At the time, neoclassical details and skylights were hidden behind curving, modernistic display cases and dioramas.

The Smithsonian's expansion into new buildings in the 1960s had a significant impact on the Natural History Museum and its contents. With the creation of the American Art Museum and the Portrait Gallery in the Old Patent Office Building, the gallery of art (which had come to the Smithsonian in 1906) finally moved out. And with the 1964 opening of the Museum of History and Technology (now the National Museum of American History), collections including domestic life, musical instruments, and cultural history—which had all fallen under the flexible rubric of the anthropology department—left the building as well.

In the last decade the museum began restoring its spectacular three-story grand halls, such as the Kenneth E. Behring Family Hall of Mammals (2003) and the Sant Ocean Hall (2008). By using space in the internal courtyards, the museum was able to provide an IMAX theater and a large cafeteria for the public in the west courtyard and a comprehensive natural history library in the east courtyard. Other renovations and additions in the last decades, such as penthouse additions to the wings for new mechanical equipment and the chiller plant located at the southeast corner of the property, have taken their inspiration from the original Hornblower and Marshall design. The 1960s windows in the west and east wings were replaced with replicas of the originals in the main building, giving a more uniform look to the entire structure. Today the Natural History Museum is the most visited of the Smithsonian museums and one of the most popular museums in the world, receiving some seven million visitors a year.

Return to the Sea (above), a special 1964 exhibit that featured some mechanically operated display units, exemplified the Smithsonian's exhibit-modernization program of the 1950s and 1960s.

The Sant Ocean Hall (left), named for donors Roger and Vicki Sant, opened in 2008. The hall has been restored to its original Beaux-Arts style, with a skylight, balconies, and a three-story-high open space. A scale model of a 45-foot-long North Atlantic right whale is suspended from the ceiling.

FREER GALLERY OF ART

The Freer Gallery of Art, the first Smithsonian museum devoted exclusively to the fine arts, was a gift to the nation from the Detroit industrialist Charles Lang Freer, a self-made millionaire. Over a lifetime he amassed the country's most outstanding private collection of Asian art. Freer's initial donation of 2,250 objects offered in 1904 was more than quadrupled by additional donations he made during the next decade. His gift also included funds for a building to house all of his collections and an endowment to support research and future acquisitions.

The son of an innkeeper, Freer (1854–1919) was born in Kingston, New York, and left school at age fourteen to work in a cement factory. His drive, ingenuity, and attention to detail—qualities that carried over into his pursuit of art—brought him great success. He earned his fortune in the manufacture of railroad cars and retired at age forty-five to dedicate himself to his art collecting.

The unparalleled Asian art collections of the Detroit industrialist Charles Lang Freer were donated to the nation to create the Freer Gallery of Art. Freer died before seeing his gift enjoyed by visitors.

Freer made many lengthy trips to China and Japan over the course of his life, visiting temples, porcelain factories, collectors, and viceroys of far-flung provinces in search of the finest works of art. His first Asian art purchase, in 1887, was a painted Japanese fan. He amassed works dating from Neolithic times to the twentieth century, including one of the world's best collections of ancient metalwork and weaponry. Among his treasures are Chinese bronzes, jades, ceramics, paintings, lacquerware, and textiles; early Buddhist sculpture; Japanese screens, Ukiyo-e paintings, and tea ceremony objects; illuminated manuscripts from the Islamic world; ancient Egyptian amulets and statuary; elaborately decorated ancient Near Eastern silver vessels; temple sculpture from Cambodia, Vietnam, and Thailand; and Mughal paintings.

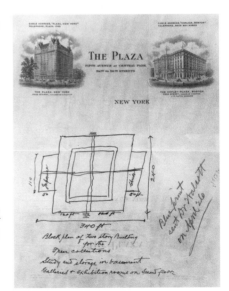

The plan for the Freer Gallery originated in a sketch drawn by Charles Freer on Plaza Hotel stationery in 1913. Freer worked with his architect, Charles A. Platt, to ensure that his vision was realized.

Freer's interest in Asian art developed as an outgrowth of his support for contemporary American artists, particularly James McNeill Whistler (1834–1903), who was profoundly influenced by Japanese artistic traditions. Freer's collection of Whistler's works is one of the largest in the world and includes the artist's only surviving example of interior decoration, the famous *Harmony in Blue and Gold: The Peacock Room*, once a private dining

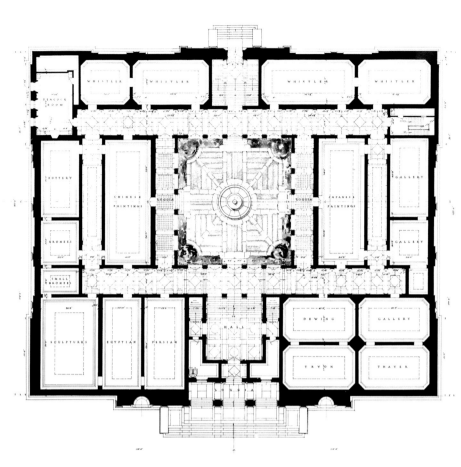

The architect's first-floor plan reflects Freer's early vision for his museum, with galleries arranged around a central courtyard.

room in London. Freer also collected the works of Thomas Wilmer Dewing, Abbott Handerson Thayer, Dwight William Tryon, and other American artists, to whom Freer was both patron and friend. Under the terms of Freer's bequest, the museum's collection of American art is not to be augmented or changed.

It was through these artists that he met the artist and landscape architect Charles A. Platt (1861–1933), whom he later commissioned to design the museum building. The two men shared a philosophy of art for art's sake—a devotion to the idea of beauty. Just as Whistler had encouraged Freer's interest in Asia, so Platt advised him on principles of classical garden design and devised a tour of Italian Renaissance gardens for him. The industrialist soon recommended Platt to his fellow business-men for various projects, such as the design of a garden for his Detroit clubhouse.

When Freer approached Platt to design his museum, he came to the architect with some definite design ideas. In an early sketch he drew for Platt on the stationery of his New York hotel, a number of the final building's key features are evident. A peaceful central courtyard, the placement of study and storage areas in the basement, and the disposition of exhibition spaces on the main floor—with Chinese galleries on one side, Japanese on the other, and American art in the interlinking spaces—were all retained by Platt in the ultimate Renaissance-inspired design.

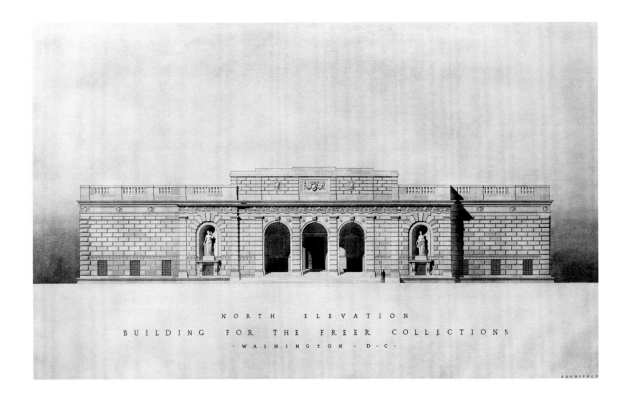

N O R T H   E L E V A T I O N

BUILDING   FOR   THE   FREER   COLLECTIONS

· W A S H I N G T O N · D · C ·

ARCHITECT

The Freer Gallery's palazzo form, round-arch doorways, sculpture niches, parapet walls, and rusticated stonework all evoke a sixteenth-century Italian Renaissance style.

The regents of the Smithsonian deliberated for two years before accepting Freer's gift in 1906. President Theodore Roosevelt, a keen advocate for the collection's acquisition, was instrumental in securing the gift. Together with a bequest of mostly European art from President James Buchanan's niece Harriet Lane Johnston, which the Smithsonian had accepted in 1906, the Freer gift was seen as the beginning of a national collection of art in Washington.

Many cities and organizations had vied for Freer's extraordinary collection, but Washington was a natural home for it. At the turn of the century—a time that elevated the idea of public citizenship—the capital was seen as a second home for Americans, and there was a great desire to beautify it as a symbol of the republic. Freer was a close friend of a fellow Michigan Republican, Senator James McMillan, who led the Senate commission dedicated to returning Washington to the classical ideals of the eighteenth-century L'Enfant Plan. Charles Platt's elegant, restrained Italianate palazzo design for the Freer fit well within the new vision for buildings that would line the Mall.

Construction of the Freer finally began in 1917, but it was almost immediately delayed because of the nation's entry into World War I. Inspired by the works of the Italian Mannerist architect Michele Sanmicheli (1484–1559), the building was faced with Stony Creek granite from Massachusetts, selected together by Freer and Platt, who each had a summer home in the western part of the state. The building consists of one principal floor, arranged around a central court, over a raised basement containing the study and storage areas. The windowless facade is enlivened with a balustraded parapet, recessed niches, and decorative friezes. The galleries are lighted by skylights of Luxfer glass, a prismatic material specially designed to provide an even display of natural light.

The new gallery was under construction in the winter of 1918. In the middle foreground can be seen the Castle's North Tower.

A recent aerial view of the Freer Gallery (above, seen from the Castle's North Tower) shows the Mall entrance and the open courtyard encircled by galleries, with skylights above. At the lower right corner is the pagoda-shaped roof of the S. Dillon Ripley International Center's kiosk entrance.

The Freer's north entrance (right) features the 1981 stone sculpture Twisted Form, by Shiro Hazami, which echoes the arched entrance. Despite the facade's simplicity, decorative ornament can be seen in a frieze and a parapet at the top of the building.

The courtyard, faced with a white Tennessee marble, was another essential element of the design from the beginning. Freer saw it as a reminder of the dynamic interaction of art and nature so integral to Asian art. The building opens onto this serene space, with its arcaded cloister and central fountain.

A classical wave-motif beltcourse wraps around the building, ornamenting the austere rusticated facade.

Because Freer's bequest included funds for study and research, the building was designed with space for a library and laboratories below ground. Today a large and steadily growing study collection is used by scholars, for laboratory analysis, and for testing conservation methods. The high basement spaces are illuminated by windows delicately inserted beneath the wave-patterned beltcourse (midlevel frieze) on the exterior.

Freer, who died four years before the museum opened in 1923, wished "to unite modern work with masterpieces of certain periods of high civilization, harmonious in spiritual and physical suggestion, having the power to broaden aesthetic culture and the grace to elevate the human mind." His gallery has long fulfilled that goal through its wide-ranging exhibition program, scholarly publications, and research. Over the years the building has not been altered; however, in conjunction with the creation of the Quadrangle, basement storage and study capacities were enlarged and an underground connection to the Arthur M. Sackler Gallery constructed in 1988.

Exhibit cases (right), shown in a skylighted gallery in the museum's first years, were specially designed and built at the Freer. During a major renovation in the late 1980s, the skylights, benches, and exhibit cases were retained and restored.

James McNeill Whistler's Harmony in Blue and Gold: The Peacock Room (1876–77)—Whistler's only extant interior design scheme—is an icon of the Freer Gallery (below). The sinuous shapes reflect the artist's amalgamation of Asian and European styles.

The elegant vaulted entrance foyer (above) features large round-arch windows that open onto a peaceful classical courtyard.

Peacocks (left) were at first kept in the courtyard to complement Whistler's Peacock Room. They were a little too noisy and dirty for the museum, however, so a new home was soon found for them at the Smithsonian's National Zoological Park.

71

NATIONAL MUSEUM
OF AMERICAN HISTORY

KENNETH E. BEHRING CENTER

The National Museum of American History opened in 1964—the culmination of years of planning and study of the most modern methods of exhibition design. It was the first Smithsonian museum to be built on the Mall since the 1920s, and in its stark modernity it was unlike any previous Smithsonian museum. One of the last major works designed by the venerable architecture firm McKim, Mead and White, the building was "classical in definition, and the detail is modern," explained the principal architect, Walker O. Cain (1915–93). "There's that peripheral parade around a very simple rectangular form that is so disarmingly simple that I think it sits in well with neo-classical buildings all around it."

The building was not only stylistically modern; it also reflected a new approach to museum presentation. In the words of Secretary Leonard Carmichael (1898–1973), the museum was designed to be "a great exhibition machine." Under its first director, Frank Taylor, who led the Smithsonian-wide exhibition modernization program at midcentury, the new museum focused on presenting an educational message using the objects as examples of their type. "If the National Museum is to accomplish its mission as defined in the broadest sense," Taylor wrote, "it must be viewed as more than a mere Trophy House—it must be accepted as a vital instrument of national education."

The stripped-down classicism and massing of the American History Museum create a colonnade effect reminiscent of the Lincoln Memorial. Cutout openings on the roof cast a "shadow cornice" on the facades, as depicted in this original rendering.

Although a museum of engineering and technology had been proposed as early as 1923, no museums had been built on the Mall since the opening of the Freer that same year. The overcrowded conditions at the Arts and Industries Building—where hundreds of objects were still displayed in a nineteenth-century style, clustered together with little written explanation—helped make the case for a modern new museum. The Smithsonian was aided as well, Taylor later said, by "the somewhat exuberant time of national pride after World War II," when "the need to describe a national museum of the history of the United States became urgent." President Dwight D. Eisenhower signed the bill on June 28, 1955, and groundbreaking for what was originally known as the National Museum of History and Technology took place three years later.

The restrained five-story rectangular building rests on a broad terraced base, much like the classical temples of Greece. This platform, which provides an on-grade entrance on the Mall, wraps around the building and steps down on the north facade to the lower grade of Constitution Avenue. The sleek Tennessee marble surfaces of alternating projecting and recessed bays evoke a kind of abstract classical colonnade. Cutouts ringing the roof level cast a geometrical silhouette on the facade that functions as a modernist "shadow cornice."

The Washington Monument can be seen from the American History Museum's Constitution Avenue elevation. The fountain in the foreground, which the architect Walker O. Cain saw as integral to the building, was once known for its display of lights and "dancing waters."

A detail of the building's "shadow cornice" shows the original windows (now blocked on the interior), which were tucked into the sides of the projecting bays.

In the museum's early years, night lighting helped emphasize the vertical windows and the walls that recalled the museum's neighbor on the Mall, the Lincoln Memorial. The underground passage was designed to hide the service entrance and museum parking.

The architect had visited several large museums in Europe and believed strongly that a museum without windows could be disorienting to visitors. He thus inserted partially hidden windows into the sides of the projecting stone-clad bays, allowing some daylight to enter the museum. With lights placed inside the recesses to shine out at night—echoing the lighted, colonnaded Lincoln Memorial to the west—the museum created a striking presence on the Mall.

Entrances for parking and the loading dock were cleverly hidden by green landscaping and by the elevation change between the Mall side and Constitution Avenue. A fountain was designed for the Constitution Avenue entrance, and two sculptures were specially commissioned for the museum: the *Gwenfritz*, by Alexander Calder (1898–1976), placed at the west end, and *Infinity*, by José de Rivera (1904–85), located on the south terrace.

Yugoslav dancers from the 1973 Smithsonian Folklife Festival assemble around the Louisiana-born José de Rivera's Infinity (1968). The specially commissioned sculpture was viewed by the museum's director, Frank Taylor, as an "essential part of the architectural concept of the museum."

Shown entering the museum shortly before its opening, the Southern Railroad 1401 locomotive (right) was intended to be visible through a window twenty-four hours a day, even when the museum was closed.

Once a popular attraction linking the two main exhibition floors, the Foucault pendulum (below)—invented by the nineteenth-century French physicist Leon Foucault to demonstrate the earth's rotation—was removed in 1998. The original Flag Hall on the floor above is visible through the oculus.

An interior exhibition hall at the time of the museum's 1964 opening illustrates the flexible gallery space that embodied the latest thinking in museum display.

More than 54,000 visitors entered the museum's gleaming stainless-steel and glass doors the first Sunday after it opened to the public on January 23, 1964. Two iconic objects in the main entry hall symbolized the museum's dual focus: the Star-Spangled Banner (history) and a Foucault pendulum (technology), which hung through an oculus to the floor below, connecting the first and second levels. The first floor was devoted to technology and science themes, such as transportation and medicine; the second floor focused on American history, with the First Ladies' gowns, political ephemera, and period domestic settings; and the third floor presented a wide range of displays—stamps and coins, printing and photography, ceramics and glass, music, and military history. Many of the collections had their own dedicated space for the first time. The musical instruments, for example, which had been tucked away on the third floor of the Natural History Museum, flourished in a new temperature-controlled gallery and performance space. As Secretary S. Dillon Ripley said, "You could just see all the instruments smiling for the first time in fifty years."

Few permanent walls interrupted the open flow of space. The plan, considered ideal by contemporary museum standards, was designed to be flexible. Importance was placed on conveying information—and visitors—in a pleasant, easily naviga-ble environment. Sleek, color-coded stainless-steel escalators transported visitors from floor to floor: blue for the west end of the building and red for the east end. Visitor fatigue was eased by the alternating use of terrazzo and wood flooring materials throughout the museum, and lounges were placed at each end, so visitors could rest while looking out at the Mall. The basement contained a public cafeteria and a snack bar, which opened onto an outdoor patio on the west side.

A gift to the Smithsonian, Julia Child's kitchen was relocated from her home in Cambridge, Massachusetts, in 2001. It is a contextual exhibit, in which an entire room is reconstructed so objects can be seen in place.

As the collections grew, the museum's spatial plan changed, and many of the original open expanses were partitioned off to form additional exhibit spaces and offices. The narrow, almost lancet-like windows of the facade's projecting bays were bricked up to limit temperature fluctuations, and four of the escalators linking the first and second floors were removed.

In 1980 the museum was renamed the National Museum of American History, signifying a shift in its focus. The change drew attention to the iconic objects of American cultural history, long associated with the Smithsonian, that were housed within: Dorothy's ruby slippers, Abraham Lincoln's top hat, the desk on which Thomas Jefferson crafted the Declaration of Independence, among many others. New storytelling exhibits, such as Field to Factory, which examined the great migration of African Americans from the South to the North in the first half of the twentieth century, explored a variety of American history narratives.

In 2001 the museum added to its name the Kenneth E. Behring Center. The building was closed in 2006 for a major renovation, with Skidmore, Owings and Merrill, the architecture firm for the Hirshhorn Museum and Sculpture Garden, hired to redesign the museum's central core. A three-story atrium, lighted from a new skylight designed to bring light into the center of the building, features a grand staircase linking the first and second floors. A new twenty-first-century exhibit space holding the Star-Spangled Banner, signaled by an abstract mirrored polycarbonate representation of the flag on the marble wall facing the atrium, has been built with the most modern conservation techniques. The renovations reflect today's style and exhibition practices.

The core of the American History Museum has been reconfigured with a new three-story central atrium, which features a grand staircase and a new exhibit on the Star-Spangled Banner. The new space features "artifact walls," showcasing objects from the collections.

SMITHSONIAN AMERICAN ART MUSEUM AND NATIONAL PORTRAIT GALLERY

The Old Patent Office Building, a National Historic Landmark, is considered one of the finest examples of Greek Revival architecture in the United States. It became part of the Smithsonian in 1958, when Congress reassigned this government building for use as the National Collection of Fine Arts (now the Smithsonian American Art Museum) and the National Portrait Gallery. Today the two are known collectively as the Donald W. Reynolds Center for American Art and Portraiture.

Construction of the Patent Office Building began in 1836, under the presidency of Andrew Jackson, and was finally completed thirty-two years later, under the presidency of Andrew Johnson. Some of the delay was caused by the Civil War, when the building was used as barracks and a hospital for wounded soldiers. Walt Whitman, who visited the soldiers here and at many other temporary hospitals across the city, called the Patent Office "that noblest of Washington buildings."

An 1851 daguerreotype (bottom left) shows Robert Mills, architect of the Patent Office Building, with his wife, Anne.

Thomas Ustick Walter (bottom right), who had a hand in the design of the Patent Office Building along with Robert Mills, is known for his dome atop the Capitol.

DONALD W. REYNOLDS CENTER
FOR AMERICAN ART AND PORTRAITURE,
OLD PATENT OFFICE BUILDING

At its completion in 1868, it was the largest building in the United States, covering more than 330,000 square feet. Many of the country's finest architects supervised its construction, including Robert Mills (1781–1855), the architect of the Washington Monument, and Thomas Ustick Walter (1804–87), the designer of the dome of the Capitol. After a disastrous fire in 1877, two wings were rebuilt by Adolf Cluss (1825–1905), the architect of the Smithsonian's Arts and Industries Building.

The entrance to the south wing of the Patent Office Building features a majestic neoclassical portico with eight fluted Doric columns. The original monumental staircase, removed in the 1930s, will eventually be reconstructed.

The south entrance hall is dominated by Robert Mills's dramatic vaulted ceiling and double staircase. The stair railing was added later by Adolf Cluss as part of his remodeling after the 1877 fire.

This monumental building in the heart of the city's commercial district takes up two blocks and comprises four wings around a courtyard. Mills was responsible for construction of the original south wing (1836–42), with its magnificent portico, using a local Aquia Creek sandstone (the same light brown stone that was used for the White House). A spectacular double curved stair led up to a soaring, groin-vaulted third-floor gallery; its 266-foot space, one of the most impressive in nineteenth-century Washington, showcased the nation's collection of patent models. This "museum of curiosities" gave the building its fame as a "temple of invention."

The next three wings were constructed in granite, a more durable material than the sandstone. The east wing (1849–55), built under Mills's supervision, housed the U.S. Department of the Interior, which included the Indian Office and the Bureau of Agriculture. The west wing (1852–57) and the north wing (1856–68) were supervised by Thomas Walter, who changed the structural framing from Mills's brick-vault masonry to a more modern system of iron beams and shallow jack-arch construction. However, these iron beams failed in the 1877 fire, and the top floors of these wings, which housed additional model halls, had to be rebuilt.

Cluss's redesign of the Model Hall (opposite and below)—with its colorful encaustic tile floor, elaborate faux-marble finishes, stained glass, and ornate iron railings—provides a striking contrast to the building's original classical austerity.

Adolf Cluss employed an exuberant "modern Renaissance" style of architecture in the reconstruction of the Model Hall and the Great Hall. These Victorian-era spaces stand in colorful contrast to the more austere classical style of the earlier construction. Skylights added to the roofs after the fire provided natural light for the upper offices and the patent galleries, and stained glass was introduced as a decorative element. Flooring became more colorful as well, with English Minton encaustic tiles laid out in geometric patterns.

The building deteriorated greatly during the first half of the twentieth century. The Patent Office moved out in 1932, after which the Civil Service Commission occupied the building until 1963. The building was threatened with demolition for a parking lot and was saved when Congress transferred the building to the Smithsonian in 1958. After extensive renovations, it was opened to the public a decade later. The building provided the first separate home for the Smithsonian's art collections, begun in 1906 and displayed first in the Arts and Industries Building and then for decades amid the Natural History Museum's skeletons and specimens. The American Art Museum, which included the first federal art collection, occupied the north side of the building. The National Portrait Gallery, on the south side, was a new initiative: it focused on telling the story of America through portraits of its people, boosted by a donation of eighteenth-century paintings from Andrew Mellon, the founder of the National Gallery of Art. The building also housed a study center, a library, and the Archives of American Art, one of the most extensive collections of artists' papers in the country. The new Smithsonian museum opened to the public in 1968, after an extensive restoration by the Washington firm Faulkner, Kingsbury and Stenhouse.

The Lincoln Gallery (above), a flexible exhibition space in the American Art Museum that retains Robert Mills's original groin vaulting, provides a contrasting backdrop for the museum's exhibitions of modern art.

An interior gallery with a maquette of the Statue of Liberty displays a variety of American artwork (left). The original marble floor was removed during restoration, and each piece was carefully numbered, stored, and cleaned before being reinstalled.

Aging infrastructure and the renewal of the Patent Office Building's neighborhood, spurred by the construction of a new city sports arena, led to another renovation in 2000. This $266 million rehabilitation, completed in 2006 by the Washington, D.C., architecture firm Hartman Cox, ushered in a new era for the building. For the first time public spaces for the two museums are integrated; a new auditorium for educational programs is located underneath the central courtyard; and systems throughout the building have been updated with state-of-the-art technology. In 2007 an undulating canopy roof of floating glass and steel, designed by the British architect Norman Foster (b. 1935) of Foster and Partners, transformed the courtyard into one of the largest interior spaces in Washington. Landscaped by Kathryn Gustafson (b. 1951) of Gustafson, Guthrie and Nicol in Seattle, the space is beautifully lighted at night.

The Patent Office Building, now one of the jewels of the Smithsonian's building collection, actually has an unusual connection to the institution's early history. Even though it did not become an official Smithsonian building until 1958, it briefly served as the first repository of the Smithsonian collections. In the 1840s, before Congress passed the act establishing the institution, the Patent Office housed James Smithson's mineral collection and his other belongings, which had come to the United States in the 1830s together with the gold coins that made up his bequest. Once the Smithsonian was chartered, it was given space in the Patent Office Building's south wing for gallery and storage use. Specimens from government-sponsored exploratory expeditions destined for the Smithsonian continued to be exhibited through the 1850s, while the Castle was under construction. It is fitting that this historic public building, restored to its most resplendent condition, is once again a temple to American creativity.

The new glass and aluminum courtyard canopy (above), which is supported by steel columns to avoid having it rest on or alter the historic structure, is illuminated at night.

Under its sinuous new canopy, the Robert and Arlene Kogod Courtyard (opposite) now features thin water scrims near the building and plantings recalling those in the nineteenth-century space.

RENWICK GALLERY OF ART

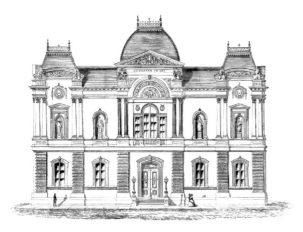

Built by the banker William Wilson Corcoran to house his personal art collection, this French Second Empire–style landmark was the first public art museum in Washington. It came into the possession of the Smithsonian in 1965 after a long and eventful history. Now, dedicated to American crafts and decorative arts of the nineteenth to the twenty-first centuries, it is a part of the Smithsonian American Art Museum. The gallery's name honors the building's architect, James Renwick Jr., who also designed the Castle, the Smithsonian's first building.

A rendering by James Renwick Jr. of the gallery's south facade features the tall mansard roofs that are hallmarks of the Second Empire style. On the opposite side of Pennsylvania Avenue, the Eisenhower Executive Office Building bears the same style.

Located across Pennsylvania Avenue from the Eisenhower Executive Office Building (originally the State, War, and Navy Building), the Renwick was neglected and then nearly demolished in the mid-twentieth century. At one point it became what the *New York Times* called " a convention hall for pigeons." Thanks to the efforts of First Lady Jacqueline Kennedy to preserve Lafayette Square and the environs of the White House, the building was saved for the nation as part of the revival of Pennsylvania Avenue.

Seven-foot sculptures by Moses Ezekiel in the arched niches represent famous artists such as Titian, Rubens, and Rembrandt. This photograph was taken about 1920, after the Corcoran Gallery had moved to its new home on Seventeenth Street.

James Renwick (1818–95) began the commission in 1859, a little more than a decade after he had won the commission for the Castle. He and Corcoran (1798–1888) had traveled together in France and took their inspiration for the building from the latest architectural style, popularized by the Emperor Napoleon III. Second Empire designs are characterized by steep mansard roofs (often crested with iron detailing), highly decorative surfaces, paired columns, and other sculptural details that project an imposing appearance. The Renwick Gallery is one of the most richly ornamented of the Smithsonian's buildings, its red brick walls embellished with paired brownstone columns and pilasters, elaborately decorated window surrounds, applied stone garlands and cartouches, and ornately carved pediments. This ornament ranges from corncob capitals on the second-floor pilasters to carved medallions with Corcoran's initials, WWC. Above the entrance in bold letters is the inscription, DEDICATED TO ART.

A profusion of rich detail on the Renwick Gallery's southwest corner includes corncob capitals on the pilasters and a medallion with the initials WWC for William Wilson Corcoran, the building's original sponsor.

As the building neared completion in 1861, at the start of the Civil War, it was taken over by the Union Army. Quartermaster General Montgomery C. Meigs (1816–92), the noted engineer responsible for the design of the Pension Building and the Washington Aqueduct, modified the structure for use as offices, inserting windows in place of blind sculpture niches on the exterior. Corcoran was a Southern sympathizer who spent the war years in France. On his return, he had difficulty reclaiming his property, but in 1869, with the help of an influential new board of trustees, he received a charter from Congress to establish a public art gallery. After extensive renovations, his Corcoran Gallery of Art, with its impressive collection of eighteenth- and nineteenth-century art and sculpture from America and Europe, opened to the public on January 19, 1874.

From the time of the gallery's restoration in the 1970s, paintings have been hung salon style in the Grand Salon, as they were in the nineteenth century.

The museum contained large interconnecting galleries on two floors, surrounding a magnificent grand staircase of mahogany. Ingenious internal light courts (now filled in) as well as skylights in the roof bathed the galleries and the staircase in diffused natural light. The most impressive gallery was the double-height Grand Salon on the second floor, which stretched some ninety-five feet across the rear width of the building. Pictures were hung salon style, one above another all across the walls. The first floor had a marble-floored palm court, which is today used as exhibit space. In 1889 an annex was built at the back of the building to house an art school.

Corcoran's collection eventually outgrew its gallery and moved down the street to a new building designed by Ernest Flagg. This new Corcoran Gallery of Art opened in 1897 (a 1928 addition was designed by Charles A. Platt, the architect of the Smithsonian's Freer Gallery of Art). Corcoran's original building was sold to the federal government in 1901. It became the U.S. Court of Claims, a role ill suited to the gallery. In its transition to office space, the building suffered from partitioning, the insertion of a steel-beam reinforcement system, and the loss of its exterior iron detail. Perhaps most damaging was the failure to protect the building from water intrusion, which decayed many of the decorative sandstone elements.

After President Lyndon Baines Johnson transferred the property to the Smithsonian in 1965, the Washington, D.C., architect Hugh Newell Jacobsen began the arduous task of restoring the building to its original use as an art gallery. The deteriorating exterior ornament was treated using the latest (and, unfortunately, untried) methods of masonry repair; this work, which involved encasing the brownstone elements in an epoxy coating, inadvertently accelerated rather than stopped the erosion. In the end, the Smithsonian was faced with faithfully reproducing all of the brownstone detail in a cast-stone material, which has held up remarkably well.

The impressive central stairway leads from the ground floor to the Grand Salon and other exhibition spaces upstairs. From the upper hall, one can look down over the marble balustrade from four sides. The ceiling's banded ornamental detail echoes the building's ebullient exterior.

The restored building, now a National Historic Landmark, was opened to the public in 1973. With the building once more filled with art, and the Grand Salon again hung salon style with tiers of pictures, the Renwick was returned to its earlier glory. "We want people to appreciate the architecture," said the first director, Lloyd Herman. "The building really is our own biggest exhibit."

Second-floor rooms accommodate craft exhibitions, such as Maria Martinez: Five Generations of Potters (1978). Here the famed Native American potter, known for her black ware, demonstrates her craft for visitors.

ANACOSTIA COMMUNITY MUSEUM

The Anacostia Community Museum, set in the lush woods of Fort Stanton Park on the east bank of the Anacostia River, not far from the Capitol, has a unique place in the Smithsonian. It was the first museum to be placed in a neighborhood, rather than with the other Smithsonian museums concentrated on the Mall. Shortly after he became secretary in 1964, S. Dillon Ripley sought a Smithsonian presence beyond the marble monuments of the institution's historic center, in order to reach out to new and underserved audiences. "We finally found our setting—a section of the city called Anacostia, along the river, full of history and life and tradition, threatened by urban blight but proud of its roots," Ripley said. "The neighborhood is, of course, what counts—the neighborhood and the strength that lies in its personalities. After some discussion, the Anacostia neighborhood group voted to ask the Smithsonian to set up their own museum. That was the beginning."

The museum's first home was the Carver Theatre (1948, John J. Zink), which was named for George Washington Carver, a noted African American agricultural researcher and teacher. After being converted to museum use, the moderne-style movie theater was opened to the public as the Anacostia Neighborhood Museum on September 15, 1967. Among the exhibits were an 1890s general store and a do-it-yourself art area. During the first year, the museum had more than 80,000 visitors.

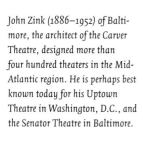

John Zink (1886–1952) of Baltimore, the architect of the Carver Theatre, designed more than four hundred theaters in the Mid-Atlantic region. He is perhaps best known today for his Uptown Theatre in Washington, D.C., and the Senator Theatre in Baltimore.

Members of the Anacostia Histor-ical Society gather in front of the museum's first home, the Carver Theatre, in 1967 (above). After the museum found a new home, the theater lay vacant for several years, but plans call for it to be renovated for a new use.

On the opening night of the Ana-costia Museum in 1967, Secretary S. Dillon Ripley stands with a group of children playing on the beloved "Uncle Beazley" (left), a fiberglass triceratops sculpture by Louis Paul Jonas. In the 1970s the sculpture was moved to the Mall but today can be found at the National Zoological Park.

The main entrance of the Anacostia Museum, nestled in the woods of Fort Stanton Park, is notable for its cylinders inset with diamonds of glass block and blue tile. A weathered-steel and stained-glass sculpture, entitled Real Justice: The Spirit of Thurgood Marshall (2004), is on loan from its sculptor, Allen Uzikee Nelson of Washington.

The museum continued to attract visitors and soon outgrew its space in the theater. A new home in Fort Stanton Park was constructed in 1984, incorporating an existing metal building erected in 1973 as a storage facility for the museum. A brick addition to the structure, including exhibit space and offices, was designed by the Washington, D.C., architecture firm Keyes Condon Florance.

In 2002 the museum undertook an unusual renovation, working with two design firms: architrave p.c. of Washington, for the public front facade, and Wisnewski Blair of Alexandria, Virginia, for the rear of the building. The two firms complemented each other well, creating a space that maximized the utility of the original building while adding features that speak to the history of African Americans. Large picture windows at the entrance and in the side galleries allow visitors ample views of the museum's leafy hilltop setting. The facade's use of red brick, in patterns suggesting a woven Kente cloth, draws on African inspiration. Flanking the entry, concrete cylinders pierced with glass block and blue tile evoke the conical towers of the eleventh-century city of Great Zimbabwe, the largest complex of ruins in Africa.

Glass, metal, and brick define the rear of the two-story building, which is designed to hold offices and other support facilities. This service portion of the museum melds seamlessly with the more colorful front facade. Most of the 1973 metal building was demolished to provide new interior space, although traces of it can still be found in the exhibition area. The design won the 2002 Vision Award from one of Washington's oldest planning groups, the Committee of 100 on the Federal City, which cited the building as "an architectural tour de force symbolizing African crafts and design."

In the museum's 28,000 square feet are a library, a research center, exhibit space, storage, and public program areas. Widely varied changing exhibitions explore aspects of African American contributions to the history of America, with an emphasis on family and community history. The museum, renamed the Anacostia Community Museum in 2006, also maintains an active presence on the Web, with an Online Academy to promote the study of African American material culture.

The African-inspired brickwork of the facade simulates the weaving of Kente cloth—one of the building's many architectural references to the heritage of African Americans.

HIRSHHORN MUSEUM AND SCULPTURE GARDEN

Joseph Hirshhorn, whose modern art collection forms the core of the Hirshhorn Museum and Sculpture Garden, called his gift "a small repayment for what this nation has done for me and others like me who arrived here as immigrants. What I accomplished in the United States I could not have accomplished anywhere else in the world." The museum's opening in 1974 represented a landmark for modern art in the capital: the fulfillment of a longstanding desire for a national museum of modern and contemporary art on the Mall. Congress had passed legislation establishing one as early as the 1930s, and a design was actually drafted by the father-and-son team of Eliel (1873–1950) and Eero (1910–61) Saarinen. The sleek, functional museum they proposed was probably too avant-garde for Washington, however, and in any case plans for its execution were abandoned in the face of World War II.

Hirshhorn (1899–1981), who was born in Latvia and came to the United States as a child, was a mining entrepreneur and a self-taught art collector and patron. In the late 1940s he sold the impressionist paintings he had collected and began focusing on contemporary art and sculpture, amassing an unparalleled collection that included major works by Thomas Eakins, Auguste Rodin, Constantin Brancusi, Henri Matisse, and many artists whom Hirshhorn befriended, such as Willem de Kooning, Pablo Picasso, Edward Hopper, and Alberto Giacometti. His collection was exceptionally strong in sculpture, much of it displayed outdoors on the vast lawns of his Connecticut home.

The Hirshhorn was constructed on the site of the original Army Medical Museum (1886), designed by Adolf Cluss. The doughnut-shaped building has a diameter of 231 feet.

Hirshhorn's art collection became the subject of intense international interest after a 1962 exhibition at the Guggenheim Museum in New York City, with museums across the United States, as well as in Italy, Israel, and Canada, vying for it. S. Dillon Ripley, then the Smithsonian's secretary, and President Lyndon Baines Johnson, who invited the Hirshhorns to the White House, successfully pressed the collector to donate his art to the nation. In 1966 Congress passed an act establishing the museum, with an outdoor sculpture garden an integral part of the design from the beginning.

As its architect the Smithsonian chose Gordon Bunshaft (1909–90), the leading designer of Skidmore, Owings and Merrill. Bunshaft had made his reputation with the ground-breaking Lever House (1952) in New York City, but it was his luminous marble Beinecke Library (1963) at Yale University that especially caught Secretary Ripley's imagination. Faced with the challenge of situating the Hirshhorn amid the monuments of the Mall, Bunshaft developed a starkly modern design that was geometrical, monumental, and, above all, sculptural—like many of the works in the donor's collection. An art collector himself, Bunshaft had strong ideas about how contemporary art should be displayed. Primary in his thinking were circulation and space flow. The cylindrical form he chose was originally to be clad in Roman travertine marble, which would have provided some stylistic relationship with John Russell Pope's classical National Gallery of Art (1941) across the Mall. Because of budget constraints, the Hirshhorn Museum was built instead using precast concrete mixed with a crushed aggregate of pink granite.

Roy Lichtenstein's Brushstroke (1996) appears to unfurl at night in front of the Hirshhorn's Mall facade. Only one window, along the third-floor balcony, punctures the structure's sleek outer shell.

97

The circular courtyard is centered on a fountain, visible to visitors through the windows above. Coffered ribs on the underside of the museum add drama to the design.

As with his Beinecke Library, which sits atop four pillars, Bunshaft envisioned the Hirshhorn floating above its plaza. Four massive piers were an essential aspect of the design. The architect drew attention to the sheer technical audacity of this feat by making the underside of the ring hold its own dramatic aesthetic interest, with deep concrete coffering creating a pattern of ribs. Bunshaft's elevated building left the plaza and the museum's nearly four-acre plot virtually open for the display and enjoyment of art. On the plaza, at the center of the ring, he placed a circular fountain, which became one of the building's signature features.

District of Columbia Mayor Walter Washington, right, presents the keys to the city to Joseph Hirshhorn on October 4, 1974, the museum's opening day (left).

Escalators in the Hirshhorn Museum's modernist glass lobby (below) whisk visitors up or down to the galleries. In 1985 a glass-enclosed gift shop was inserted here to provide more gallery space on the lower level— the only major alteration to the original museum.

The eighty-two-foot-tall building is entered from Independence Avenue through a glass lobby containing escalators to carry visitors up and down. A basement and three floors of public exhibition space above ground offer some 60,000 square feet of exhibition area, while the top floor is reserved for staff offices. Carpeted galleries rim the museum's outer ring; an internal ovoid-shaped ring contains terrazzo-floored corridors, with sculpture displays and benches for visitors. The inner walls are curtains of glass that look out onto the central courtyard and the fountain. On the third floor a balcony offers a panoramic view of the Mall; from the exterior this appears as a slit-eye window, the only rupture in the facade's monumental severity.

Exterior, windowless galleries hold works that are sensitive to light, while the glass-walled, courtyard-facing gallery displays sculpture (opposite and below). Floor-to-ceiling windows overlook the courtyard.

Bunshaft wanted to emphasize the special location of the museum, halfway
between the Washington Monument and the Capitol. The Hirshhorn lies at the
southernmost end of a key north-south axis developed in L'Enfant's original plan
for the city and reinforced in the 1901 McMillan Plan; this axis also takes in the
National Gallery of Art's sculpture garden, the National Archives, and the Old
Patent Office Building. To underscore this axis, Bunshaft proposed a sunken
sculpture garden running across the Mall, featuring a 350-foot-long reflecting
pool surrounded by walkways and outdoor sculpture. Although the plan generated intense controversy over the possibility that the historic vista between the
Capitol and the Washington Monument might be disrupted, it was approved by
city and federal authorities. Tremendous public opposition developed, however,
and plans for construction were halted.

The sculpture garden was eventually built as a much smaller sunken plot close
to the museum, following a 1971 proposal by Benjamin Forgey, then the architecture critic of the *Washington Star*. The austere, pebble-surfaced garden was
reconfigured in 1981 by the prominent landscape architect Lester Collins
(1914–93), providing wheelchair access, lush areas of lawn, shade and ornamental trees, and additional plantings. The plaza around the building was likewise
redeveloped, with further plantings and parterres added in 1993 by James Urban

and Associates, a landscape design firm in Annapolis, Maryland. In 2008 the museum acquired the sculpture *For Gordon Bunshaft*, by Dan Graham (b. 1942), a fitting tribute to the architect that was placed in the garden.

The sculpture garden was not the only controversial aspect of the Hirshhorn design. The building itself represented such a dramatic departure from earlier buildings on the Mall that it provoked extremely strong reactions at the time of its opening in 1974. While Paul Goldberger of the *New York Times* praised the circular plan and its "pleasant processional sequence," his famous colleague, Ada Louise Huxtable, called the building "born-dead, neo-penitentiary modern." Backlash also arose against the donor and the idea of erecting a memorial on the Mall to a living person. Yet as time passed, these controversies receded. In 1981 the *Washington Post* hailed the redesigned sculpture garden as a "jewel-like park within a park."

In its mission to explore and engage the arts and artists of today, the Hirshhorn Museum has greatly expanded on Joseph Hirshhorn's original bequest. The museum created a black-box space in the basement for exhibiting video and other new media art; it has commissioned many new pieces for its permanent collection, and it supports a wide-range of temporary shows, experimental projects, and artist retrospectives. As Secretary Ripley said at the time of the opening, "The purpose of the Hirshhorn is to remind us all that life is more than the usual, that the human mind in its relentless diversity is capable of seeing life subjectively, and being stirred by objects into new and positive ways of thought, thus escaping from the numbing penumbra of the ritual known as everyday."

The Hirshhorn's stark geometry creates a streamlined backdrop for the bronze sculptural group Last Conversation Piece *(1995), by Juan Muñoz.*

NATIONAL AIR AND SPACE MUSEUM

The National Air and Space Museum opened on July 1, 1976—as part of the Bicentennial of the United States—to thrilled visitors. A series of dramatic alternating masses of marble and glass, the building features exhibition spaces that show airplanes suspended against the natural backdrop of the sky. "It's probably the only place in the world where people can walk through a real spacecraft," said the museum's first director, the Apollo 11 astronaut Michael Collins. At the dedication, President Gerald R. Ford declared the museum "America's birthday gift to itself." And the *Washington Post* heralded the opening as "A Bicentennial Blast-Off for a Wonder of Marble and Glass." The *New York Times* architecture critic, Ada Louise Huxtable, was more tongue-in-cheek when she wrote, "It's a bird, it's a plane, it's Supermuseum!" and called the museum "a cross between Disney World and the Cabinet of Dr. Caligari." The building and its contents continue to enthrall visitors today.

This 1917 Quonset hut in the South Yard behind the Castle, originally used by the U.S. Signal Service, became the home of the National Air Museum's early air and space collection.

The Smithsonian has been collecting objects associated with flight ever since the tenure of its third secretary, Samuel P. Langley, an astronomer who competed (unsuccessfully) with the Wright Brothers in the quest for the first manned flight. Langley's Great Aerodrome of 1903, which was built in a shed in the South Yard behind the Castle, is now on display at the Air and Space Museum's Steven F. Udvar-Hazy Center. In 1928 Charles Lindbergh presented the institution with the world's most famous plane, the *Spirit of St. Louis*, and in 1948 the Wright Brothers' 1903 Flyer found its permanent home at the Smithsonian as well.

The only building large enough at the time to house these objects was the Arts and Industries Building; above the exhibits of presidential china and the like, planes were hung from the roof trusses as if in midflight (see page 47). Once the space program began, rockets were given to the Smithsonian, and these—too large of course for the building—were displayed outside, along what became known as Rocket Row. Many of the air and space objects were also exhibited in an old World War I Quonset hut in the Castle's South Yard. In 1946 Congress formally established the National Air Museum. Twenty years later, as the space race captured the nation's imagination, Congress authorized $40 million for the construction of a major new building on the Mall to house the museum.

The Smithsonian awarded the commission to the St. Louis–based architecture firm Hellmuth Obata and Kassabaum for the challenging project—a building on the historic Mall that could handle both enormous objects and enormous crowds. Gyo Obata (b. 1923), the principal designer, studied for a time at the Cranbrook Academy of Art in Michigan under the Finnish architect Eliel Saarinen, whose son Eero designed Dulles International Airport (1962). "When I went to Cranbrook to study with Eliel Saarinen," Obata reminisced, "he taught me not to be afraid of large projects, of the planning involved and so forth. Learning about community, urban planning and the relationships of buildings to each other was a very important part of my learning and an important inspiration to me."

An architectural rendering of the Air and Space Museum from 1972 illustrates how its marble-clad masses alternate with glass and steel-framed voids.

Obata was challenged to design a museum near the foot of the Capitol that would fit in with the classical grandeur of the Mall, while creating an architectural statement that reflected the modernity of space exploration. The architect carefully studied the axial relationship of the site to the National Gallery of Art's original building and the Hirshhorn Museum. By varying the massing, the design "prevented an overly monolithic effect," he noted, adding that the blocks' "recesses align with projecting portions of the National Gallery's south elevation as if the buildings might fit together like two pieces of a puzzle." His 636,000-square-foot building comprises four sections clad in the same Tennessee marble used for the National Gallery's West Building. The marble alternates between glass in three recessed exhibit bays; flooded with even, north-facing light, these glass areas feature heavy truss systems to support the planes suspended above. Window walls were placed at each end of the building as portals to bring in large artifacts; the one at the west end is still active. The building's large-format IMAX theater was the first one built in Washington, D.C.

The glass wall at the building's west end can be removed to accommodate the movement of large exhibit objects.

The jewel-like 1988 restaurant addition on the museum's east end (above) features panes of glass that complement the original building and is connected to the main building by a glass vestibule.

Alejandro Otero's Delta Solar (1977) was a gift to the museum from the people of Venezuela (right). The stainless-steel panels of this sculpture move gently in the breeze.

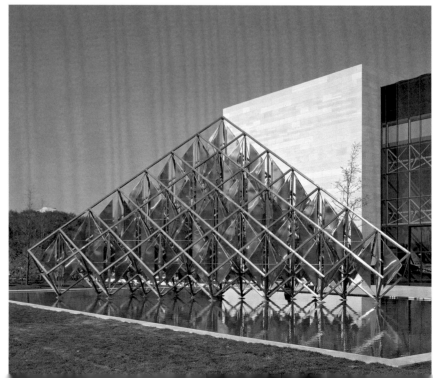

Over the years the building has been little changed. In 1988 the museum returned to the original architects to design a large restaurant at the building's east end. This elegant, geometrically shaped glass structure, which complements the trusses and the glass in the original building, could be said to resemble a lunar landing vehicle. In 2000 the building's skylights, which had been executed in acrylic plastic as a cost-cutting measure, were replaced with glass, as Obata had intended. At the same time, the museum's window glass was replaced with slightly tinted glass to better protect the objects. New perimeter vestibules were also added to the north and south entrances, providing an extra layer of climate control between the outside elements and the exhibits.

The grounds of the museum are also graced with several sculptures, an important element of the museum's overall appearance. *Delta Solar*, a triangular-shaped stainless-steel sculpture evoking sails, created by the renowned Venezuelan artist Alejandro Otero (1921–90), is set in a water feature at the west end of the building. Facing the Mall at the museum's south entrance is *Continuum*, a work depicting the cosmos by the American sculptor Charles O. Perry (b. 1929). The third sculpture, at the north entrance, is by Richard Lippold (1915–2002): *Ad Astra* (Latin for "to the stars"), notable for its delicate starbursts and slim vertical tapers. The artworks—evoking images of rockets, jet streams, wings, antennae satellites, planes, balloons, gliders, and other air and space vehicles—hint at the collections that await visitors inside. Within the museum, the history of space exploration is captured by *The Space Mural: A Cosmic View*, by Robert T. McCall (b. 1919).

Sculptural bollards—appropriately wing shaped—provide an unobtrusive security element at the museum's north entrance.

The National Air and Space Museum remains one of the most popular in the world. In 2007 *Architectural Record* and the Harris Interactive Poll named it one of America's one hundred favorite buildings. But as airplanes and spacecraft grew exponentially larger than the vehicles from the dawn of the space age, the need arose in the late twentieth century for larger quarters in which to display them. No land was available on the Mall or in downtown Washington, so the Smithsonian ventured out to Fairfax County, Virginia, for a twenty-first-century–sized facility.

At the center of the Air and Space Museum is the popular Milestones of Flight Gallery. The glass curtain wall and the skylights offer the sky as a backdrop for the aircraft.

Charles Lindbergh's famous airplane, the Spirit of St. Louis (above), was relocated to the Milestones of Flight Gallery from the Arts and Industries Building, where it had hung since 1928.

Alan B. Shepard Jr. examines the Freedom 7 spacecraft after his Project Mercury suborbital space flight in 1961 (right). The craft was then located at the National Air Museum in a Quonset hut in the South Yard behind the Castle, but it was later moved to the new Air and Space Museum.

Rockets on display in the museum are easily accommodated in the vast interior galleries (opposite). Viewing platforms and stairs allow visitors to see from all angles.

STEVEN F. UDVAR-HAZY CENTER

To develop the Steven F. Udvar-Hazy Center as part of the National Air and Space Museum, the Smithsonian returned once more to Helmuth Obata and Kassabaum. This new facility in Chantilly, Virginia, nestled between the eighteenth-century Sully Plantation and Eero Saarinen's mid-twentieth-century Dulles International Airport, houses the largest aviation and space artifacts in the Air and Space collection. Named in honor of its major donor, who is the owner of one of the world's largest aircraft-leasing companies, it opened in December 2003.

The mammoth Udvar-Hazy Center contains three main components: the barrel-ceilinged Boeing Aviation Hangar, the James S. McDonnell Space Hanger, and a 164-foot-high observation tower; the latter, reminiscent of an airport control tower, is named in memory of Donald D. Engen, who died in a gliding accident in 1999 while he was director of the Air and Space Museum. In addition to approximately 130 aircraft, 150 space artifacts, and more than 1,500 smaller objects, Udvar-Hazy also contains a 479-seat IMAX theater, classrooms, offices, and visitor amenities. The center's landscaping includes the sculptural *Space Exploration Wall of Honor* outside the building's main entrance and the 70-foot work *Ascent*, by the Virginia sculptor John Safer (b. 1922).

An aerial view of the Steven F. Udvar-Hazy Center of the National Air and Space Museum (above) shows the entire complex and reveals how one section interlocks with another.

A covered walkway leads to the Space Exploration Wall of Honor and John Safer's Ascent (opposite), two sculptural elements commissioned for the building.

Taut, brushed-steel cladding resembling aircraft skin covers the Udvar-Hazy Center (below). In the middle is the Donald D. Engen Observation Tower, and to the right is the IMAX theater.

Samuel P. Langley's Great Aerodrome (1903) is suspended from the roof of the Udvar-Hazy Center as if in flight.

The Boeing Aviation Hangar, which encompasses nearly 300,000 square feet, recalls the immense hangars constructed in the early twentieth century to house dirigibles. It is so enormous that the entire National Air and Space Museum on the Mall could fit inside it. The aircraft on exhibit, suspended from twenty-one steel trusses (each of which holds up to 20,000 pounds), can be viewed from several vantage points: on the ground and at eye level on a series of catwalks surrounding the hangar. "When we hang the craft, we try to show them in positions or at angles that capture their spirit or purpose," explains William "Jake" Jacobs, an exhibit designer. Air ducts are cleverly curved to blend with the trusses, and the railings around the exhibit areas and catwalks of both hangars are punctuated at intervals by benches, so visitors can rest and enjoy the space. To protect the artifacts, both the aviation and space hangars were designed using a minimum of natural light. The Boeing Hanger is illuminated by a clerestory window, while the 53,067-square-foot James S. McDonnell Space Hangar, which contains the 1976 space shuttle *Enterprise*, has a darkened ceiling evocative of outer space.

For conservation of the Smithsonian's air and space artifacts, the Air and Space Museum has operated a storage facility in Suitland, Maryland, since 1952. A series of simple prefabricated metal huts, it is named the Paul E. Garber Preservation, Restoration and Storage Facility. Garber (1899–1992) joined the Smithsonian in 1920 and was instrumental in assembling the nucleus of the museum's aeronautical collection. For many years, the Garber facility was open on a limited basis so visitors could see much of the 90 percent of the collection that was not on display on the Mall.

To consolidate the museum's entire conservation program in Virginia, plans are now under way for the creation of a new hangar at the Udvar-Hazy Center. This modern facility will be named in honor of Donald Engen's late wife, Mary Baker Engen. When the Mary Baker Engen Restoration Hangar is completed, the entire Udvar-Hazy Center will cover approximately 760,000 square feet. Visitors will be able to see restoration work in progress, as well as more of the Air and Space Museum's collections than have ever been shown before.

A side view of the Boeing Aviation Hangar shows the wide doors that open to move large aircraft. The structure recalls the enormous 1930s dirigible hangars at Moffat Field, near Sunnyvale, California.

The Concorde, donated by Air France, fits easily into the mammoth Boeing Aviation Hangar. Walkways at the left provide an eye-level view of the exhibits.

Cooper-Hewitt National Design Museum

In 1976 the Smithsonian opened a museum devoted to design in the former New York City home of the steel magnate and philanthropist Andrew Carnegie (1835–1919). The Upper East Side mansion, the namesake of its neighborhood, the Carnegie Hill Historic District, is now filled with more than 250,000 objects—ranging from textiles and wall coverings to drawings, prints, applied arts, and furniture. Carnegie's daughter, Margaret, suggested that her father's "heart would sing" to know that his home was open to the public.

The mansion was designed at the turn of the twentieth century in the style of a Georgian country house by the New York architecture firm Babb, Cook and Willard. The architects were known for their grand residential estates on Long Island, as well as for office buildings such as Montreal's first skyscraper, the New York Life Insurance Building (1887). Carnegie, unlike other wealthy architecture patrons such as the Astors and the Vanderbilts, did not seek to make an especially grand statement. He told his architects that he desired "the most modest, plainest and roomiest house in New York." The location he selected, on northern Fifth Avenue, was then considered to be almost wilderness, but it provided his wife, Louise, with ample space for a garden. Construction began in 1901, the year Carnegie sold his Carnegie Steel Company to the United States Steel Corporation. He devoted the rest of his life to philanthropic efforts, in particular the establishment of free public libraries in the United States and his native Scotland.

Louis Comfort Tiffany's influence is visible in the scalloped-glass canopy at the main entrance to the Cooper-Hewitt Museum.

The sixty-four-room house, built at a cost $1 million, may not have been modest or plain, but it certainly was roomy, and it incorporated modern technology. Although the four-story building appears to be built of brick with limestone trim, it actually features a structural steel frame. Steel skeletons were making possible the earliest skyscrapers at this time; Carnegie's mansion was the first private residence in New York City to use this pioneering technology—a choice that was especially fitting, given that Carnegie had made his fortune in steel. The house had one of the first residential Otis passenger elevators (now in the Smithsonian's National Museum of American History), and it also boasted an artesian well, its own generator, central heating, and a unique air-conditioning system.

The elegant Georgian-style Carnegie mansion (left), located on Manhattan's Upper East Side, is faced with smooth limestone blocks and decorative detail. It now houses the Cooper-Hewitt National Design Museum.

A historic conservatory as well as a pergola-like structure designed by Polshek and Partners connect the mansion to the Miller-Fox townhouses of the Cooper-Hewitt Museum (below).

Elaborate plasterwork, photographed shortly after the museum opened, surrounds this room, which features a parquet floor and a brilliant chandelier. Potted plants, popular in Edwardian-era home decor, evoke the ambiance of the turn of the twentieth century.

Large fans in the attic pulled air in from outside through cheesecloth filters in the basement, over tanks of cooling water, and then into every room. Brass-and-copper coal-fueled boilers manufactured by Babcock and Wilcox, the country's leading boiler company (which was at that time installing the boilers to power New York's new subway system), were housed in a hygienic white-tile room. Still visible today are the miniature railroad tracks on which the coal car traveled to convey fuel from the 250-ton coal bin to the furnace.

The house is entered through a portico with a copper and leaded-glass canopy, designed in the style of Louis Comfort Tiffany. Past the marble vestibule, the main hall and ceiling are paneled in Scottish oak, in deference to Carnegie's ancestry, and the floor is a rare tropical monkey wood. Every morning the Carnegies were awakened at 8:00 A.M. by the sound of the eminent organist Walter C. Gale performing on the house's enormous Aeolian organ, located off the main hall. Although the organ is long gone, remnants can still be seen. Carnegie loved the instrument so much that he donated more than eight thousand organs to churches, civic institutions, and schools. The first floor contained the main suite of entertaining rooms: a formal drawing room, a dining room, and an ornately decorated and gilded music parlor. It also featured Louise Carnegie's conservatory, an indoor garden with a special small furnace, as well as Andrew Carnegie's sitting room overlooking Central Park (now the gift shop).

A grand Scottish oak stair leads to the second floor, which once housed the Carnegie family's bedrooms, dressing rooms, and sitting rooms. The library, with its teak trim and cabinets, was designed by the noted plein-air painter and interior

designer Lockwood DeForest (1850–1932). These rooms are now all exhibition galleries for the Cooper-Hewitt Museum. They retain many of their original architectural features, such as carved mantels, ornate plasterwork, and elaborate wood door surrounds. The third floor was used for guest rooms and the fourth for servants' quarters. Today these upper floors provide a variety of expanded gallery areas and support spaces.

All of the house's principal rooms were designed to face the large garden at the rear. Once paved with walkways of Vermont granite that have since been replaced by concrete, the garden was the pride of Louise Carnegie. Surrounded by a wrought-iron fence and stone posts, it contained azaleas, wisteria, rhododendron, crab apple and chestnut trees, and a rock garden she designed herself. There was even a playhouse for daughter Margaret.

After Carnegie died in 1919, his widow continued to live in the house until her death in 1946. It was then turned over to the Carnegie Corporation and leased to the Columbia University School of Social Work, which undertook renovations for its offices. In 1968 the collections and the library of the Cooper Union Museum for the Arts and Decoration (which had been founded in 1897 by the granddaughters of the industrialist Peter Cooper as part of Cooper Union for the Advancement of Science and Art) were transferred to the Smithsonian with the stipulation that they remain in the city. A solution was found in the Carnegie mansion, which was leased to the Smithsonian by the Carnegie Corporation and then in 1972 donated along with an adjacent townhouse on East 91st Street. Secretary S. Dillon Ripley spoke at the time of "the need for a museum showcase, in which an endlessly rich variety of historical decorative arts material can be drawn upon, utilized and enjoyed." He proposed that "the Smithsonian can be influential in offering guidelines to more beautiful designs in every day life."

Stained glass was a popular decorative element in grand homes such as the Carnegies' mansion (top left). This window with a garland and a lyre overlooks the garden.

In the music room (top right), each corner showcases different musical instruments, such as intertwined violins, to represent the Carnegies' love of music.

The New York architecture firm Hardy Holzman Pfeiffer, known for its renovation of the Brooklyn Academy of Music and other historic buildings, adapted the mansion for use as a museum, retaining most of the interior's character, especially on the first and second floors. The building opened to the public as the Cooper-Hewitt Museum of Design and Decorative Arts in October 1976, with some five thousand visitors a week lining up around the block to see the opening exhibit, MAN trans-FORMS, conceived by the Austrian architect Hans Hollein (b. 1934).

The museum faces many challenges in displaying within the confines of a historic house a growing collection dedicated to design. To provide additional space for offices, classrooms, and other programmatic uses, two townhouses were acquired at 9 East 90th Street and 11 East 90th Street. In 1996 the Cooper-Hewitt undertook a major renovation with Polshek and Partners, another noted New York City firm known for its design of the Rose Planetarium and the restoration of Carnegie Hall. The museum's front entrance was made accessible, the two adjacent townhouses were rehabilitated, and a connector was built to link the mansion to the townhouses, using a style reminiscent of a garden pergola. The Babcock and Wilcox boiler system had to be dismantled, but because of its historical importance, the front face of the boilers was reassembled in a new location in the basement. The rest of the mechanical equipment was disbursed to museums throughout the country.

In 2000 further renovations were carried out in the mansion, which is now a National Historic Landmark. The fourth floor was then converted into a storage facility for the prints and drawings collection, which forms one of the largest decorative arts and design archives in the world. Future plans for the museum call for gallery expansion on the third floor and the relocation of office and support areas within the mansion and the two townhouses.

The Angel Cage was designed by Arata Isozaki, a Japanese architect, for the opening exhibition MAN transFORMS in 1972 (above). Conceived by another architect, Hans Hollein, the exhibition effectively used the mansion's historic spaces.

Decorative arts and design collections are displayed in the historic mansion (opposite). Among them are two historic bentwood chairs: the Fully Elastic Armchair (1808) by Samuel Graggon, on the left, and a bentwood rocker (ca. 1860) by Michael Thonet, on the right.

THE QUADRANGLE

The elegant Enid A. Haupt Garden sits in the center of the Quadrangle complex, bounded by some of the Smithsonian's most historic buildings: the Castle, the Arts and Industries Building, and the Freer Gallery of Art. It spreads across 4.2 acres, with courts and contemplative corners variously evoking a traditional Persian garden, a Chinese water garden, and an ornate Victorian parterre—creating a dialogue between East and West. Despite its grandeur, it is in a sense only a roof garden. Beneath this placid scene is an immense sunken structure housing the National Museum of African Art, the Arthur M. Sackler Gallery, and the S. Dillon Ripley International Center. Three separate pavilions in the garden lead to the two underground museums and the education center.

Jean-Paul Carlhian, architect of the Quadrangle complex, traveled the world to gain inspiration for his underground design.

The collection of the African Art Museum was amassed by Warren M. Robbins (b. 1923), a foreign service officer, who displayed it beginning in 1964 in a Capitol Hill rowhouse where Frederick Douglass once resided. Robbins founded the museum to teach Americans the value of African art and culture. Now a leading center for the study and display of ancient and contemporary African visual arts, it became a part of the Smithsonian by a 1979 act of Congress. Arthur M. Sackler (1913–87), the donor of the Sackler Gallery, was a research doctor and a philanthropist with a lifelong interest in collecting art. His 1982 gift to the Smithsonian included a thousand outstanding Asian and Near Eastern works of art and funding for a building, forming a perfect complement to the Freer collection.

The desire to place the Sackler Gallery near the Freer, coupled with the lack of open space on the Mall, drove the selection of the utilitarian South Yard behind the Castle as the site for the new museum complex. The Quadrangle opened to the public in 1987, following a complicated planning, design, and construction phase lasting nine years. Recalling a historic design feature of many English and American colleges and universities, the Quadrangle also reflects in its name Secretary Ripley's vision for the Smithsonian as a university open to all the world—a place for scholars, students, artists, and families to come together.

A number of architects and landscape architects contributed to the Quadrangle. In 1978 the Japanese architect Junzo Yoshimura (1908–97), a figure greatly admired by American art patrons and revered in his own country, developed the concept of a discreet building located within and largely under a garden. Shepley, Bulfinch, Richardson and Abbott, the oldest continuously operating American architecture firm, was retained in 1980 to shepherd the project through the historic preservation and design review process and to oversee construction.

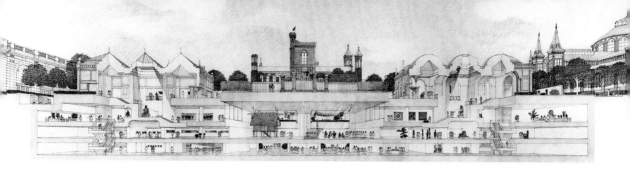

In response to comments by the U.S. Commission of Fine Arts and the National Capital Planning Commission, Jean-Paul Carlhian (b. 1919), principal architect for Shepley, Bulfinch, significantly reworked the design. He recast the project to harmonize the new facilities with the existing landmark buildings of the Mall. From the strong colors and Victorian skylines of the Castle and the Arts and Industries Building, he developed the pyramidal roofs of the Sackler Gallery and the reddish hue of the African Art Museum. From the arch and wave motifs of the limestone Freer Gallery, he adopted the warm gray granite color of the Sackler and the rounded domes of African Art. The third garden structure, a round pagoda-like pavilion that provides the entrance to the Ripley Center, was adapted from a drawing by the great English garden designer Humphry Repton (1752–1818).

The Quadrangle complex, as shown in this architectural rendering, is almost fully underground, except for the entrance pavilions to the three facilities. The Sackler Gallery, the African Art Museum, and the S. Dillon Ripley International Center can be accessed from the lowest (third) level without going outside.

In a 1984 construction photograph, workers are shown laying concrete underground. Extreme care was taken to protect the Smithsonian's three nearby historic structures—the Castle, the Arts and Industries Building, and the Freer Gallery of Art.

121

The Sackler Gallery's pyramidal roofs were designed to complement the Smithsonian's Arts and Industries Building, while its color was inspired by the nearby Freer Gallery of Art.

Nearly 96 percent of the Quadrangle lies underground. The engineering and design were extremely challenging, because one-third of the complex sits below the city's water table. Concrete slurry walls, a construction technique developed in Carlhian's native France, were used to build the foundations. The engineers had to account for the weight of the garden's several feet of damp earth and its cast-concrete water features.

Great care was taken to create a graceful descent into the underground facilities. The pavilion entrances have soaring ceilings and huge windows that frame vistas of the garden and the Castle. Carlhian wanted to avoid the association of going down into a "bargain basement" or an underground garage, so he suffused the stairways of the two museums with light from stained-glass windows—amber for the Sackler and blue for African Art—as well as from clear glass skylights in the roof. Each stairway was given its own distinctive design, echoing the forms of the roofs—curved for African Art and diamond-shaped for the Sackler. And at the bottom of each stair is a sparkling water effect, reflecting the light from above.

Circular and octagonal motifs in the African Art Museum's double stairway (opposite) recall the African-inspired domes that visitors first see outside.

A grand stairway leads from the Sackler's entrance down into the museum spaces. Triangular motifs in the skylight and the window reflect the pyramidal roofs of the entrance pavilion.

The kiosk entrance to the Ripley Center takes its pagoda-like design from eighteenth-century English garden follies. Its small size gives no indication of the enormous three-story complex underneath.

The limestone spiral stairway for the entrance pavilion to the Ripley Center is equally dramatic. For a model the designers looked to the famous Renaissance chateau of Blois in France. Many team sessions in the Boston offices of Shepley, Bulfinch were devoted to understanding this stair's geometry. Halfway down, the visitor arrives at a shallow circular space lined with short, swelling columns, where the path swings around toward the concourse. Deliberately low and dark, this domed vestibule offers a dramatic contrast to the soaring, light-filled concourse below that serves all facilities. Lined with abstract classical motifs and crossed by bridges three stories above, this hall directs visitors to exhibitions and numerous classrooms.

A trompe-l'oeil mural by Richard Haas at the east end of the underground concourse depicts a crumbling classical facade, with a glimpse of the Castle above. Through the arch is a representation of the Arts and Industries Building.

The concourse connects class-rooms, offices, and museums. Skylights and extensive plantings bring a sense of the outdoors to the underground space.

The Haupt Garden is a remarkable oasis in the city, especially if one remembers the South Yard when it contained work sheds and a parking lot. Enid A. Haupt (1906–2005), the publishing heiress and horticulture patron who funded it, requested mature specimen trees, saying that she was "getting on" and wanted to be able to enjoy the garden. The landscape designer Lester Collins (who was also involved in the reworking of the Hirshhorn Sculpture Garden) was brought in to consult on the plant selection. The African Art section features water effects evocative of North African–influenced designs in Andalusia. The Sackler garden, with its pink granite moon gates, was inspired by the Temple of Heaven in Beijing. The central parterre virtually replicates the Victorian garden created behind the Castle for the Bicentennial in 1976. Nineteenth-century lampposts and the Smithsonian's collection of historic cast-iron garden furniture, urns, and wickets are scattered throughout the garden. The red sandstone gates at the Independence Avenue entrance to the garden are based on James Renwick's unexecuted original design; they were carved by Constantine Seferlis (1930–2005), a local stone carver who also worked on the Washington National Cathedral. Marrying old and new, the Renwick gates provide an elegant and appropriate entryway to the hidden treasures of the Quadrangle complex.

At the center of the Quadrangle is the Enid A. Haupt Garden (above) on the south side of the Castle. The above-ground entrance pavilion of the Sackler Gallery is at left, and the African Art Museum pavilion is at right. The circular kiosk entrance of the S. Dillon Ripley International Center can be seen at the far left.

Expansive views of the Haupt Garden, including a star-shaped planting (opposite), are available from large picture windows in the pavilion entrance of the African Art Museum.

NATIONAL POSTAL MUSEUM

The National Postal Museum opened in 1993 in the imposing Beaux-Arts building just off the Mall that for almost all of the twentieth century served as the main post office for the city of Washington. Depressions in the lobby floor, where people stood in line at the teller windows, are still visible. Completed in 1914, the post office was designed by the firm of Daniel Burnham of Chicago. Burnham, who died in 1912, was also responsible for the adjacent Union Station, which had opened in 1908. These buildings formed part of a monumental three-part composition that the architect envisioned as a classical entranceway to the capital, centered on Union Station. The third building, meant to frame the train station on the eastern side—as the post office does on the western side—was finally built in 1992: the Thurgood Marshall Federal Judiciary Building, designed by Edward Larrabee Barnes (1915–2004).

At the beginning of the twentieth century, train travel dominated the country's transportation system. It was also the most efficient means of delivering the mail. Placing the post office next to the station meant that the two could be linked easily by rail, speeding up the processing of mail. In towns all across the nation, post offices were being similarly situated near railroad stations.

The National Postal Museum is located in the neoclassical building near Union Station that originally served as the city's main post office. An Ionic colonnade runs along its facade.

Many of the historic lobby's original features—the coffered ceiling, torchères, bronze chandeliers, and ornate plasterwork (as seen in a 1914 view, left)— were recreated after being lost in subsequent decades.

The restored lobby (below) leads to the National Postal Museum. Because the original marble proved too costly to recreate, the torchères are now in bronze.

The neoclassical architecture of Burnham's post office building reflects the City Beautiful movement, which dominated American design in the century's early years. Proponents sought to use beauty and classical order to help ameliorate the problems of urban living at a time of tremendous social upheaval. The movement had its origins in the monumental neoclassical buildings of Chicago's World's Columbian Exposition of 1893, famed for its so-called White City. Under Burnham, Washington, D.C., became one of the great exemplars of this progressive movement; he headed the McMillan Commission of 1901, which reimagined the Mall as a grand open space, harkening back to L'Enfant's original plan for the city. Burnham also helped design the dome of the Smithsonian's Natural History Museum (see pages 19 and 58), which was intended to serve as a model for future buildings in the capital.

The style fell somewhat out of favor in the years after World War I, and by the 1950s the original post office interior had been heavily modernized to suit the times. Fluorescent lighting replaced the marble torchères, plastic laminate countertops were added, and a low ceiling was installed to create a mezzanine for air-conditioning ducts and other utilities, destroying much of the original coffered ceiling in the lobby. Today this grand space has been restored with the reconstruction of the coffered ceiling and the ornamental plasterwork, the installation of replica chandeliers, and replacement of the torchères (now in bronze rather than marble), all of which provide an impressive setting for the entrance to the National Postal Museum.

The museum, which has one of the largest collections of stamps in the world, was created in 1990 by an agreement between the Smithsonian and the U.S. Postal Service. It had its origins in the National Philatelic Collection, which was started at the Smithsonian in 1886 and first housed at the Arts and Industries Building and later at the National Museum of American History.

The museum exhibitions are located in the area behind the public lobby. This part of the building, once the mail-processing and distribution section, was never seen by the public visiting the city post office. The Washington-based firm Florance Eichbaum Esocoff King was the architect for the museum part of the building renovation. (The renovation of the entire building, which is managed by the U.S. General Services Administration, was undertaken by the local architect Shalom Baranes.) The building itself still houses government offices.

Many postal-themed elements were incorporated into the museum's interior design. The baluster detail on the escalators takes its inspiration from a cancellation mark. A silkscreened stamp design, featuring the famous 1901 Empire Express upside-down stamp, appears on the entrance hall ceiling. In the principal central space of the museum are envelope-design tiles in the flooring, and the light fixtures recall the rural towers used by postal pilots to make mail drops. This light-filled atrium, from which the museum's various galleries extend, creates an outstanding setting for the stories told here about the creation of the postal system and the movement of the mail in the United States.

With its vaulted ceiling and its colonnade, this exhibit installation, entitled Business of the Mail: Parcel Post, reflects the building's neoclassical architecture.

NATIONAL MUSEUM
OF THE AMERICAN INDIAN

Best known for the expressive, undulating building that opened on the Mall in 2004, the National Museum of the American Indian is actually housed in three architecturally distinct buildings in three locations. In 1989 Congress authorized the creation of this museum in Washington, D.C., as part of the Smithsonian complex. The act stipulated that the collection of the Museum of the American Indian in New York City, which had been founded seven decades earlier by George Gustav Heye, be transferred to the Smithsonian. Because the museum was an important part of New York's cultural history, the Smithsonian agreed to retain a presence in the city, while moving the bulk of the Heye collection to Washington. In New York the museum, which needed new quarters, was established in the historic U.S. Custom House at Bowling Green, near the foot of Manhattan. In the Washington area, two new buildings were planned: a prominent museum on the Mall and a structure dedicated to storage and conservation in suburban Suitland, Maryland.

The Smithsonian wanted to ensure that Native Americans in the United States were engaged in all aspects of the museum, especially the programming and the design. The noted Philadelphia architecture firm Venturi Scott Brown arranged a series of consultations with Indian tribes throughout the United States, Canada, and Central and South America to determine essentials for the museum. Many thoughtful comments came from the tribes interviewed: "Say who we are visually." "A living museum—not formal and quiet." "We want to welcome people—that should be in the entrance." "A huge skylight to give the sense of the sky." The consultation process resulted in a voluminous program document, "The Way of the People," intended to inform the architects of what Native Americans wanted in the museum.

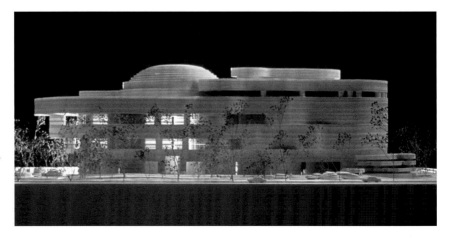

A preconstruction model of the American Indian Museum underscores the prominence of circular forms, which were designed to resemble rock formations found in the North American landscape.

It was crucial that the designs for the two new buildings embody and communicate the museum's mission: to represent and interpret Indian culture as living and vibrant for all audiences, native and non-native. There are no generic Indian building types, but there are commonalties. Traditional native ways of building are highly responsive in their forms, materials, and technologies to diverse climatic and site conditions and social structures. The two new structures had to convey these considerations while respecting the existing architecture and environments of their selected sites.

The design process for the National Museum of the American Indian on the Mall was unlike that undertaken for any other Smithsonian museum. Douglas Cardinal (b. 1934), a member of the Canadian Blackfoot tribe, partnered with the Philadelphia architecture firm Geddes Brecher Qualls Cunningham for the project. Cardinal organized a three-day "vision session" in Washington in 1995, inviting tribal elders, who blessed the site of the future museum, as well as Native American artists and others. Critical design ideas emerged from the session—for example, the building's entrance should face east, toward the rising sun; the museum should contain as much natural material as possible; and it should be welcoming to everyone. Cardinal believed that the new building "should endeavor to be a spiritual act and should demand from all those contributing to the design and construction the very best of their endeavors." He assembled a team of Native Americans to work with him on the design, among them a landscape architect, a botanist, and a weaver.

The oculus in the ceiling above the Potomac, the 140-foot-high gathering place at the American Indian Museum, emphasizes the importance of the sky to Native American cultures. A flowing staircase echoes the building's undulating forms (above and opposite).

The final building undulates with sensuality, its curving walls drawn from studies of earth and rock formations eroded by time. The facade's rough-hewn Kasota limestone, which contains fossils in the blocks nearest the base, gradually becomes smoother as it reaches the top of the building. Constructed with an interior of poured-in-place concrete slabs, the 443,000-square-foot structure is five stories above grade, with a basement. The masklike main entrance on the east end is framed with steel trusses that cantilever outward to form a canopy. This end of the building carries out an unusual dialogue with the Capitol, which it faces, including the Capitol's topmost statue *Freedom* (1863, Thomas Crawford), which wears a Native American headdress. A low, stepped dome on the museum complements the dome of the National Gallery of Art across the Mall. Its oculus, which opens up to the sky to bring in sunlight, serves as an interior focal point above the museum's central gathering space, called the Potomac (the Piscataway word for "Where the goods are brought in").

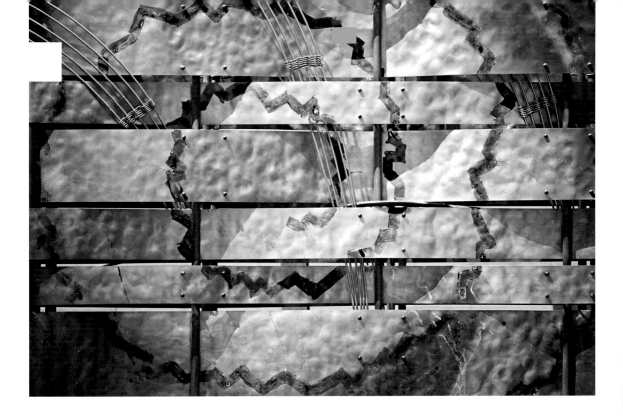

Throughout the exterior and the interior, the sacred circle is a dominant form: the building contains more than a thousand curves and almost no straight walls. Each design element emphasizes an aspect of Native American traditions. The Potomac, the building's welcoming center, is named for the capital's river and is full of architectural symbolism. The floor is laid with a circle of local red Seneca sandstone (the same material used for the Castle), surrounded by a ring of granite and maple flooring, all of which is set in quadrants and separated by metal strips aligned with the directions of the compass. A wall designed as a patterned copper screen wraps around the area. All of the interior spaces use colors and themes from Native American landscapes and decorative motifs reflecting Native American food and culture.

The exterior landscaping includes plants indigenous to areas of Indian culture. Water, an important element, flows around three sides of the building. More than forty granite boulders surround the museum. These "elders," or "grandfather rocks," signify ancestors of Native Americans.

Although Douglas Cardinal left the project before construction began in 1999, his Native American design team worked with Polshek and Partners, Smith Group, Jones and Jones, and the Native American Design Collaborative to finish the building. Consultations with Native Americans continued throughout the construction process. To celebrate the opening of this living museum, the building was launched in September 2004 with a week of festivities, attended by more than 20,000 Indians from tribes across North and South America.

Abstract motifs in a copper-screen wall (above) evoke traditional Native American basket-weave and textile patterns. The screen was designed by Ramona Saki-estewa, a Hopi weaver from Santa Fe, New Mexico, who also created the color schemes for the museum's interiors.

The gift shop (opposite), which includes exhibits, reflects the architectural curves that are an integral design element of both the interior and the exterior of the American Indian Museum.

CULTURAL RESOURCES CENTER

The first of the two Washington buildings to be designed and built was actually the Cultural Resources Center, which was needed to store the Heye collection of artifacts from New York, as well as to provide conservation facilities and a

research center. Its site in nearby Suitland, Maryland, is a wooded area not far from the Smithsonian's Museum Support Center, home to other storage and conservation facilities. The architecture firm Polshek and Partners of New York City (responsible for the 1996 renovation of the Cooper-Hewitt National Design Museum) was selected to design the new structure in partnership with the Native American Design Collaborative and Tobey and Davis. Construction of the 164,000-square-foot building began in 1996 and was completed in fall 1998. Its radial steel roof in a nautilus shape references many Native American forms, such as cone-shaped tipis and medicine circles; it also expresses circular movement, almost like a tribal dance.

The unusual, nautilus-shaped roof of the Cultural Resources Center in Suitland, Maryland, was one of the first elements that emerged from a design workshop with the architects. This model shows how the roof recalls Native American forms from tipis to dance circles.

Because the collection contains many objects sacred to Native Americans, with different tribal customs for their handling, it was important that this new facility be a place that would not only store the objects using proper climate controls but also respect the objects' significant role in Native American life. Special handling areas and ceremonial spaces are located both outside and inside, so that tribes can use their objects in private. Storage rooms are designed to place the most sacred objects nearest the ceiling—closer to the sky. Staff describe the Suitland center as the heart and soul of the museum, a place where the collections have found a respectful home.

At the entrance to the Cultural Resources Center (left), the building's solid steel roof becomes a glass-filled fretwork canopy.

An exterior view of the Cultural Resources Center entrance (opposite) obscures the swirled roof. Native plantings surround the building, which is located in a wooded area.

The Alexander Hamilton U.S. Custom House (right) in New York City is the home of the George Gustav Heye Center of the National Museum of the American Indian. The building's architect, Cass Gilbert, won the 1899 design competition for it—besting his mentors, the firm of McKim, Mead and White.

Located in the former cashier's office of the Custom House, the Heye Center's Resource Center (below) has an original iron cage and light fixtures that were restored during the 1980s renovation.

GEORGE GUSTAV HEYE CENTER

When the new National Museum of the American Indian was authorized in 1989, the Alexander Hamilton U.S. Custom House—a glorious Beaux-Arts building completed in 1907—lay vacant and crumbling. Designed by the renowned architect Cass Gilbert (1859–1934), the mammoth 450,000-square-foot structure is a symphony of ornament and architectural detail. It is announced at the entrance with the figures *The Four Continents,* by Daniel Chester French (1850–1931), sculptor of the seated Abraham Lincoln in the Lincoln Memorial. The building's interior contains many surprises, such as Guastavino-tile vaulting (like that found at the National Museum of Natural History), 1936 murals of New York Harbor by the Works Progress Administration artist Reginald Marsh (1898–1954), and sumptuous spaces indicative of the building's former use as the headquarters of the Port of New York.

This National Historic Landmark had been saved from the wrecking ball in 1979 by Senator Daniel Patrick Moynihan of New York. All it lacked was a good use. The need to find a New York presence for the new American Indian Museum proved an excellent solution. The basement and the first and second floors were leased to the Smithsonian by the U.S. General Services Administration. The New York architecture firm Ehrenkrantz, Eckstut, and Kuhn worked with the Smithsonian to design the space and conduct a complete exterior and interior restoration.

Special care was taken to insert the George Gustav Heye Center into this historic fabric. The modern exhibit galleries, for example, were designed as windowless "black boxes," behind which the historic architectural finishes and the original windows are protected. Varied temporary and permanent exhibitions are augmented with extensive public programming, including music, dance, and film.

After beginning his collecting in his early twenties, Heye (1874–1957) amassed the largest private collection of Native American artifacts in the world. The son of a German immigrant who made his fortune in petroleum, Heye first worked as an investment banker. In 1916 he founded the Museum of the American Indian in New York, serving as its director until 1956.

His vast collection, transferred to the Smithsonian in 1989, forms the core of the National Museum of the American Indian. The objects come from virtually all tribes of the United States, as well as from most of those in Canada and a significant number from Central and South America and the Caribbean. Together they offer a vivid window into the traditions and cultures of Native American life in the Western Hemisphere. The three buildings that make up the museum, which evolved in a consultative process unique in the Smithsonian's history, provide a rich environment for the diverse cultural collections they contain.

The Diker Pavilion of Native Arts and Culture in the Custom House opened in 2006. Echoing the building's central rotunda, the elliptical-shaped pavilion is a performance space with glass exhibit cases along the walls, featuring objects from the Heye collection.

RESEARCH CENTERS

Research is at the core of the Smithsonian's mission, as laid out by James Smithson—"the increase and diffusion of knowledge." In addition to the behind-the-scenes areas of the museums, where many laboratories and study centers are located, the institution maintains several research centers, mostly scientific, that are world renowned. Located throughout the Western Hemisphere, these research centers boast buildings as rich and varied as the research that is conducted within.

SMITHSONIAN ASTROPHYSICAL OBSERVATORY

The Smithsonian has been a pioneer in astrophysics for more than a century. As early as 1870, Secretary Joseph Henry expressed a desire to have an observatory on the Smithsonian grounds. His wish was fulfilled by the third secretary, Samuel P. Langley, who established the Smithsonian Astrophysical Observatory in 1890 in a simple wooden shed in the Castle's South Yard. In the observatory's early days, several field stations were set up to augment the facility in Washington. Like the temporary shed behind the Castle, these field stations were small, rudimentary structures, located in desolate areas of Arizona, New Mexico, California, Egypt, Chile, Iran, and South Africa.

In 1955 the Smithsonian and Harvard University entered into a partnership, after which the observatory's headquarters was moved to Cambridge, Massachusetts. In 1968 another observatory was opened, on Mount Hopkins, Arizona, today known as the Fred Lawrence Whipple Observatory. An astronomer, Whipple (1906–2004) was the director of the Smithsonian Astrophysical Observatory from 1955 to 1973. The facility named for him represented a radical departure from the traditional observatory design of a telescope located

inside an enclosed domed structure. The Whipple Observatory introduced the Multiple Mirror Telescope, a computer-controlled telescope mount with six individual telescopes that functioned as one, greatly increasing the power of observation and setting a new standard for telescope design. This telescope was replaced in 1999 with newer technology, but the building still retains much of its original character.

The Fred Lawrence Whipple Observatory on the summit of Mount Hopkins, Arizona, was opened in 1968 as a facility of the Smithsonian Astrophysical Observatory. The Multiple Mirror Telescope was encased in a boxlike structure. The building itself turned with the telescope mount.

The most recent addition to the Smithsonian's family of astrophysical observatory facilities is the Submillimeter Array at the summit of the Mauna Kea volcano in Hawaii, 13,386 feet above sea level. This complex telescope system is located near Hilo, where the institution constructed an 18,000-square-foot operations and support facility, designed by Urban Works, Incorporated, of Honolulu, on the grounds of the University of Hawaii. The station features the world's first imaging interferometric telescopic at submillimeter wavelengths, measuring millimeter and submillimeter radiation—the light of colors not visible to the human eye—in order to study the birth and death of stars.

The Earl S. Tupper Research and Conference Center in Panama City (top left) is the administrative heart of the Smithsonian Tropical Research Institute.

Once the Tivoli Hotel kitchen, the small building on the left is all that remains of the former hotel (top right), which was demolished in 1975. The kitchen is now used by the Tropical Research Institute as part of the Tupper Center.

The plain wooden and concrete interior of the 1916 Ancon Building (right) reflects its tropical location in Panama, including transom doors and wooden shutters to keep out the hot sun and the rain. Some of the institute's offices were eventually relocated to the new Tupper Center nearby.

Involved in marine science since the late nineteenth century, the Smithsonian is now one of the leaders in the field of biological diversity. Its Tropical Research Institute, a collection of sites located on both coasts and in the middle of the Republic of Panama, developed as an outgrowth of the 1910 Smithsonian Biological Survey of the Panama Canal Zone. The architecture here is rich and varied. The buildings—such as the two-story visitors center on Barro Colorado Island (see page 27), built in the 1920s as the institute's first laboratory—reflect the center's tropical location: louvered windows, verandas, and a mixture of wood and concrete predominate. The simplicity of these buildings' vernacular designs belies their functionality in humid climates.

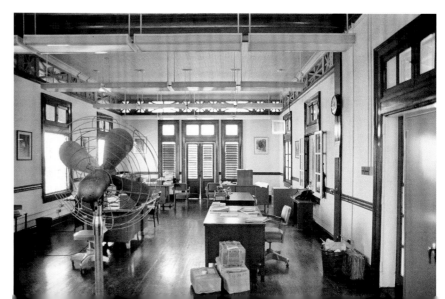

When the Canal Zone was returned to Panama under the 1977 treaty with the United States, several former U.S. military buildings were acquired by the institute and converted into offices, exhibit space, and laboratories. The Italianate-style Ancon Building of 1916, originally part of the Gorgas Army Hospital in Panama City's Ancon area, was attached to the hospital's former mortuary and had a fully equipped operating room. "My office for twenty-five years or so," one scientist remarked, "was the chemical lab with drains in the floor."

The institute's administrative center is the Earl S. Tupper Research and Conference Center, located on Ancon Hill. The building, which includes a library, a lecture hall, laboratories, and offices, was designed by the Panamanian architect Octavio Mendez Guardia and dedicated in 1989. It was built on the site of the historic 1906 Tivoli Hotel, where visitors came to view the construction of the Panama Canal. The hotel was demolished in 1975 because of termite infestation, but a small one-story building once used as a kitchen remains and is in use as offices.

In 2003 the institute opened a new laboratory at its field station Bocas del Toro on Panama's Caribbean coast. Designed in a tropical style by the firm Kiss and Cathcart of Brooklyn, New York, the building champions sustainable design elements. The solar roof, for example, collects rainwater, provides shade, and produces most of the laboratory's electricity.

Planning is under way to consolidate some of the research facilities and incorporate land recently purchased in the nearby town of Gamboa, founded in 1916 for the workers of the Panama Canal dredging operation.

The modern laboratory building in Bocas del Toro, Panama, features a solar roof with an overhang in the tropical style.

CARIBBEAN CORAL REEF ECOSYSTEMS PROGRAM

Simple wooden structures, pastel in color, fit their tropical location at the Caribbean Coral Reef Ecosystems Program at Carrie Bow Cay, Belize (opposite, top).

This laboratory, located at Carrie Bow Cay on one acre of the Belize Barrier Reef, was established in 1972. A part of the National Museum of Natural History, it serves as a research base for scientists working across the region. The architecture on this small island mirrors its tropical location, with structures integrated among palm trees, white beaches, and the azure sea. Small, pastel-colored colonial-style buildings, with corrugated metal roofs and timber siding, are raised on stilts to allow for water flow and ventilation.

SMITHSONIAN MARINE SCIENCE STATION

The Tyson House (opposite, bottom) is a modern version of the tropical vernacular architecture prevalent at the Smithsonian Marine Science Station. Designed by the Florida architect Peter Jefferson (b. 1928) in 1977 for Peter and Jeanne Tyson, it was relocated from Vero Beach, Florida, to the station in Fort Pierce as a gift from the owners.

Created in 1969, this station in Fort Pierce, Florida, is dedicated to the study of south Florida's ecosystems and biodiversity. It has evolved from its first home on a World War II–vintage floating barge to an eight-acre campus. Its structures for research, storage, and administration are designed in a simple tropical style, like those of the Smithsonian's other tropical facilities.

SMITHSONIAN ENVIRONMENTAL RESEARCH CENTER

Devoted to the study of the Chesapeake Bay watershed, this center in Edgewater, Maryland, is located on 2,700 acres of land adjacent to the Rhode River, a subestuary of the Chesapeake Bay. Originally a 365-acre dairy farm, the property was bequeathed to the Smithsonian in 1964. Only the cow barn, which today serves as the library, survives from the original farm. More than twenty modest buildings are scattered around the property. Future plans include construction of a new housing center and additional research facilities. In 2007 the ruins of the eighteenth-century Java Plantation and surrounding property were acquired by the research center, preserving the area's rich history.

The gable-roofed Reed Educational Center is the largest building at the Smithsonian Environmental Research Center. Located on a Chesapeake Bay subestuary in Edgewater, Maryland, it is a modern version of the eighteenth-century colonial architecture prevalent in this rural area.

MUSEUM SUPPORT CENTER

With more than 137 million objects and specimens, the Smithsonian's collections are so extensive and diverse that only 2 percent can be displayed to the public at any given time. Objects were originally stored in each museum, but because the collections expanded much more rapidly than the buildings, off-site storage had to be found. One curator at the Natural History Museum devised a plan to draw attention to the overcrowded conditions: in response to his director's request for a specimen to decorate the office, he delivered a stuffed African rhinoceros.

As it planned for expansion in the 1960s, the Smithsonian recognized that the space on the Mall should be dedicated primarily to public access and that research and storage should be located off site. Property was found six miles from the Mall, in Suitland, Maryland, adjacent to the World War II–era Quonset huts of the Paul E. Garber Preservation, Restoration and Storage Facility of the National Air and Space Museum.

The Smithsonian's innovative Museum Support Center, authorized by Congress in 1975 and opened in 1983, was designed by the Washington, D.C., firm Metcalf/KFC. Covering 4½ acres of land abutting a wooded area, the center is made up of a series of rectangular storage buildings in precast concrete, known as pods. The original 524,000-square-foot four-pod structure was designed in a zigzag shape to enable additions without compromising the design concept. To protect the different collections, the pods were built with climate control and

The innovative storage pods at the Museum Support Center in Suitland, Maryland, are illustrated in this architectural rendering. The center was designed expressly to allow for growth without compromising the original design.

storage units in all shapes and sizes. Opposite the pods is a smaller building that mirrors the form of the pods and houses offices and research facilities. The support center also serves as the home of the Smithsonian's pioneering Museum Conservation Institute, the center for research in and conservation of the institution's collections. The two buildings are connected by a covered walkway, which provides two points of access to the complex, one for visitors and one for items in the collection—keeping the objects separate from circulation corridors and adding an additional layer of protection to the site. The center is near the Suitland Parkway, a scenic drive constructed during World War II to connect military installations between what are now Andrews and Bolling Air Force Bases.

In 2007 a fifth pod, covering some 120,000 square feet, was opened. Designed by the Philadelphia firm Ewing Cole in keeping with the original pod design, it houses the Natural History Museum's "wet collection" (specimens preserved in alcohol).

At the time of its opening, the Museum Support Center received accolades as the "World's Most Perfect Attic." Representing the latest in museum storage technology, it has served as a model for museums throughout the world.

Serving as both a storage facility and a conservation laboratory, the Museum Support Center opened in 1983 with the four pods seen here. Visible at the top is the Paul E. Garber Preservation, Restoration and Storage Facility of the National Air and Space Museum.

CHRONOLOGY

The dates given indicate the starting and ending years of design and construction of the museum buildings.

1838–68
Old Patent Office Building
(Donald W. Reynolds
Center for American Art
and Portraiture)

1847–55
The Castle

1859–74
Renwick Gallery of Art

1879–81
Arts and Industries Building

1889–present
National Zoological Park

1890–present
Smithsonian
Astrophysical Observatory

1901–3
Cooper-Hewitt
National Design Museum

1902–7
George Gustav Heye Center,
National Museum
of the American Indian

1903–11
National Museum
of Natural History

1911–14
National Postal Museum

1917–23
Freer Gallery of Art

1923–present
Smithsonian Marine Science
Network (Tropical Research
Institute, Caribbean Coral
Reef Ecosystems Program,
Marine Science Station,
Environmental Research
Center)

1957–64
National Museum
of American History
(Kenneth E. Behring Center)

1967–74
Hirshhorn Museum
and Sculpture Garden

1968–2002
Anacostia
Community Museum

1972–76
National Air
and Space Museum

1977–87
The Quadrangle (National
Museum of African Art,
Arthur M. Sackler Gallery,
S. Dillon Ripley International
Center, Enid A. Haupt Garden)

1983–present
Museum Support Center

1995–2004
National Museum
of the American Indian,
Mall Building

1996–98
Cultural Resources Center,
National Museum of the
American Indian

2000–2003
Steven F. Udvar-Hazy
Center, National Air and
Space Museum

DIRECTORY

Anacostia Community
Museum
1901 Fort Place S.E.
Washington, D.C.

Arts and Industries Building
900 Jefferson Drive S.W.
Washington, D.C.

The Castle
1000 Jefferson Drive S.W.
Washington, D.C.

Cooper-Hewitt National
Design Museum
2 East 91st Street
New York, New York

Freer Gallery of Art
12th Street and
Jefferson Drive S.W.
Washington, D.C.

Hirshhorn Museum
and Sculpture Garden
Independence Avenue
at Seventh Street S.W.
Washington, D.C.

Museum Support Center
4210 Silver Hill Road
Suitland, Maryland

National Air and Space
Museum
6th Street and Independence
Avenue S.W.
Washington, D.C.
including the
Steven F. Udvar-Hazy Center
14390 Air and Space
Museum Parkway
Chantilly, Virginia

National Museum
of American History
(Kenneth E. Behring Center)
14th Street and Constitution
Avenue N.W.
Washington, D.C.

National Museum
of Natural History
10th Street and Constitution
Avenue N.W.
Washington, D.C.

National Museum
of the American Indian
4th Street and Independence
Avenue S.W.
Washington, D.C.
including the
Cultural Resources Center
4220 Silver Hill Road
Suitland, Maryland
and the
George Gustav Heye Center
1 Bowling Green
New York, New York

National Portrait Gallery
*(Donald W. Reynolds Center for
American Art and Portraiture)*
8th and F Streets N.W.
Washington, D.C.

National Postal Museum
2 Massachusetts Avenue N.E.
Washington, D.C.

National Zoological Park
3001 Connecticut
Avenue N.W.
Washington, D.C.
*(with a facility in Front Royal,
Virginia)*

Old Patent Office Building
*(Donald W. Reynolds Center for
American Art and Portraiture)*
8th and F Streets N.W.
Washington, D.C.

The Quadrangle
*(including the Arthur M. Sackler
Gallery, Enid A. Haupt Garden,
National Museum of African
Art, and S. Dillon Ripley Inter-
national Center)*
1100 Jefferson Drive S.W.
Washington, D.C.

Renwick Gallery of Art
17th Street and
Pennsylvania Avenue N.W.
Washington, D.C.

Smithsonian
American Art Museum
*(Donald W. Reynolds Center for
American Art and Portraiture)*
8th and F Streets N.W.
Washington, D.C.

Smithsonian Institution
Building *(The Castle)*
1000 Jefferson Drive S.W.
Washington, D.C.

RESEARCH CENTERS
(open by appointment)

Carribean Coral Reef
Ecosystems Program
Carrie Bow Cay, Belize

Smithsonian
Astrophysical Observatory
60 Harvard Street
Cambridge, Massachusetts
*(with facilities in Arizona
and Hawaii)*

Smithsonian Environmental
Research Center
647 Contees Wharf Road
Edgewater, Maryland

Smithsonian Marine
Science Station
701 Seaway Drive
Fort Pierce, Florida

Smithsonian Tropical
Research Institute
Roosevelt Avenue
Balboa, Ancon, Panama

SELECTED BIBLIOGRAPHY

Of the many books and publications about the Smithsonian, the following are just a few. The institution has an excellent Web site (www.si.edu), on which each museum and research center is listed with information about its history. More detailed histories and photographs can be found on the Web sites of the Smithsonian Institution Archives (www.siris.si.edu) and the Office of Architectural History and Historic Preservation (www.si.edu/ahhp).

THE CASTLE

Field, Cynthia R., Richard E. Stamm, and Heather P. Ewing. *The Castle: An Illustrated History.* Washington, D.C.: Smithsonian Institution Press, 1993.

Hafertepe, Kenneth. *America's Castle: The Evolution of the Smithsonian Building and Its Institution, 1840–1878.* Washington, D.C.: Smithsonian Institution Press, 1984.

ARTS AND INDUSTRIES BUILDING

Beauchamp, Tanya Edwards. *From Germany to America: Shaping a Capital City Worthy of a Republic. Historic Preservation Solutions for Adolf Cluss Buildings, 1962–2005.* Washington, D.C.: Adolf Cluss Exhibition Project, 2005.

Lessoff, Alan, and Christof Mauch, editors. *Adolf Cluss, Architect: From Germany to America.* Oxford, England, and New York: Berghahn, 2005.

NATIONAL ZOOLOGICAL PARK

Ewing, Heather. "The Architecture of the National Zoological Park," in *New Worlds, New Animals: From Menagerie to Zoological Park in the Nineteenth Century.* Baltimore: Johns Hopkins University Press, 1996.

Mergan, Alexa. "From Bison to BioPark: 100 Years of the National Zoo." Washington, D.C.: Friends of the National Zoo, 1989.

NATIONAL MUSEUM OF NATURAL HISTORY

Field, Cynthia R., and Jeffrey T. Tilman. "Creating a Model for the National Mall: The Design of the National Museum of Natural History," in *Journal of the Society of Architectural Historians,* 63 (March 2004), 52–73.

Yochelson, Ellis. *The Natural History Museum: 75 Years in the New National Museum.* Washington, D.C.: Smithsonian Institution Press, 1985.

FREER GALLERY OF ART

Lawton, Thomas, and Linda Merrill. *Freer: A Legacy of Art.* Freer Gallery of Art. New York: Harry N. Abrams, 1993.

Morgan, Keith N. *Charles A. Platt: The Artist as Architect.* Architectural History Foundation. Cambridge, Mass.: MIT Press, 1985.

NATIONAL MUSEUM OF AMERICAN HISTORY

Cain, Walker O. (architect), interview with. www.si.edu/ahhp.

Wilson, Richard Guy. "High Noon on the Mall: Modernism versus Traditionalism, 1910–1970," in *Studies in the History of Art,* 30 (1991), 142–67.

SMITHSONIAN AMERICAN ART MUSEUM/NATIONAL PORTRAIT GALLERY (Donald W. Reynolds Center for American Art and Portraiture), Old Patent Office Building

Evelyn, Douglas. *A Public Building for a New Democracy: The Patent Office Building in the Nineteenth Century.* Ann Arbor, Mich.: University Microfilms, 1997.

Robertson, Charles J. *Temple of Invention: History of a National Landmark.* Smithsonian Institution. London and New York: Scala Publishers, 2006.

RENWICK GALLERY OF ART

Reynolds, Donald. *Nineteenth and Twentieth Century Architecture*. New York: Cambridge University Press, 1992.

ANACOSTIA COMMUNITY MUSEUM

Hutchinson, Louise Daniel. *The Anacostia Story: 1608–1930*. Washington, D.C.: Smithsonian Institution Press, 1977.

HIRSHHORN MUSEUM AND SCULPTURE GARDEN

Fletcher, Valerie. *A Garden for Art: Outdoor Sculpture at the Hirshhorn Museum*. Washington, D.C.: Hirshhorn Museum, 1998.

Krinsky, Carol Herselle. *Gordon Bunshaft of Skidmore, Owings & Merrill*. Architectural History Foundation. Cambridge, Mass.: MIT Press, 1988.

NATIONAL AIR AND SPACE MUSEUM

Ezell, Lin. *Building America's Hangar: The Steven F. Udvar-Hazy Center*. Washington, D.C.: National Air and Space Museum, in association with D. Giles Limited, London, 2004.

Kudalis, Eric. *Gyo Obata*. Minneapolis: Capstone Press, 1966.

McMahon, Michael. "The Romance of Technological Prowess: A Critical Review of the National Air and Space Museum," in *Technology and Culture* (1981).

Obata, Gyo, and Hellmuth Obata and Kassabaum. *Gyo Obata, 1954–1990*. Tokyo: Eando Yu, 1990.

COOPER-HEWITT NATIONAL DESIGN MUSEUM

Dolkart, Andrew S. *Cooper-Hewitt National Design Museum: The Andrew and Louise Carnegie Mansion*. London and New York: Scala Publishers, 2002.

THE QUADRANGLE

Park, Edwards, and Jean-Paul Carlhian. *A New View from the Castle: Arthur M. Sackler Gallery, National Museum of African Art, S. Dillon Ripley Center, Enid A. Haupt Garden*. Washington, D.C.: Smithsonian Institution Press, 1987.

NATIONAL MUSEUM OF THE AMERICAN INDIAN

Blue Spruce, Duane, editor. *Spirit of a Native Place: Building the National Museum of the American Indian*. Washington, D.C.: National Geographic Press, 2004.

Cardinal, Douglas, and Jeannette Armstrong. *The Native Creative Process*. Penticton, British Columbia: Theytus Books, 1991.

SMITHSONIAN RESEARCH CENTERS

Abbott, C. G. *An Account of the Astrophysical Observatory of the Smithsonian Institution, 1904–1953*. Washington, D.C.: Smithsonian Institution, 1966.

Royte, Elizabeth. *The Tapir's Morning Bath: Mysteries of the Tropical Rain Forest and the Scientists Who Are Trying to Save Them*. New York: Houghton Mifflin Company, 2001.

THE MALL

Field, Cynthia R., and Nathan Glazer. *The National Mall: Rethinking Washington's Monumental Core*. Baltimore: Johns Hopkins University Press, 2008.

Longstreth, Richard W., editor. *The Mall in Washington, 1791–1991*. Washington, D.C.: National Gallery of Art, 1991.

Penczer, Peter R. *The Washington National Mall*. Arlington, Va.: Oneonta Press, 2007.

GENERAL

Ewing, Heather. *The Lost World of James Smithson*. New York: Bloomsbury, 2007.

Lubar, Steven, and Kathleen M. Kendrick. *Legacies: Collecting America's History at the Smithsonian*. National Museum of American History (Kenneth E. Behring Center). Washington, D.C.: Smithsonian Institution Press, 2001.

Park, Edwards. *Treasures of the Smithsonian*. Washington, D.C.: Smithsonian Institution Press, 1983.

Ripley, S. Dillon. *The Sacred Grove*. New York: Simon and Schuster, 1969.

ACKNOWLEDGMENTS

We are especially grateful to the Smithsonian Women's Committee and to the Office of Planning and Project Management for providing the funding necessary to publish this book. We also thank the Contributing Membership for their enthusiastic support of the Smithsonian and are delighted that this book has been selected as a gift for them.

Much appreciation goes to Sheryl Kolasinski, director of the Office of Planning and Project Management, and to the current and former directors of the Office of Architectural History and Historic Preservation, Sharon C. Park and Cynthia R. Field, for their contributions to the text and their encouragement and support.

Clara Rosenman has been a volunteer with the Office of Architectural History and Historic Preservation for more than ten years. She was instrumental in locating many of the photographs and establishing a database of photographs that greatly assisted our selection.

We also thank Rick Stamm, curator of the Smithsonian Castle Collection, for his guidance and good humor throughout the project, and Harry Rombach, associate director for facilities master planning, for his technical expertise and good will.

There are not enough words to express our thanks to Smithsonian Photographic Services and the wonderful photographers throughout the institution. Simply put, without them this book would not exist. Many of the contemporary photographs, including the cover photograph, were taken by Ken Rahaim, whose enthusiasm and artistic vision enhanced our understanding of the Smithsonian's architectural treasures. We thank Michael Barnes and John Dillaber for doggedly tracking down negative numbers and photographs and for their patience.

We are also grateful to Hal Aber, Mark Avino, Larry Bird, Jessie Cohen, Justin Estoque, Karen Fort, Cynthia Frankenburg, Lizanne Garrett, Mark Haddon, Carl Hansen, Don Hurlbert, Melissa Keiser, Betsy Kohut, Mike Lang, Jennifer Morris, Mehgan Murphy, Jim O'Donnell, Fernando Pascal, Dane Penland, Nancy Pope, Klaus Ruetzler, Lou Stancari, and others who had a hand in gathering the photographs. Photographer Eric Long deserves special thanks for his invaluable assistance with last-minute photography and assistance.

A large percentage of the photographs in the book are used courtesy of the Smithsonian Institution Archives. We are grateful to the staff, especially archivist Ellen Alers, and we particularly thank the institution's historian, Pamela Henson, for her time, assistance, and encouragement and for the outstanding database of historic Smithsonian images (available to the public on www.siris.si.edu) that the Institutional History Division has created.

This book is a collaborative effort involving our colleagues throughout the institution. David Bohaska, Cecilia Chin, Kelly Crawford, Roy Clarke, Pedro Colon, Tom Crouch, Steve di Girolamo, Jon Gibbons, Trish Graboske, Shannon Graham, George Gurney, Von Hardesty, David Hogge, Holly Laffoon, Susan Ostroff, Ray Rye, Michael Shawver, David Shayt, Janice Slivko, Michelle Spofford, Mary Augusta Thomas, Robert Vogel, and Helena Wright are among the many who shared their knowledge. We thank each and every one of them.

We also thank Lisa Nichols of Goetz Printing in Alexandria, Virginia; Joel Sanders of Esto Photographics in Mamaroneck, New York; Peter Penczer; Photos Plus, Washington, D.C.; and Michelle Pointon of Visual Images Photographs in Silver Spring, Maryland, for their assistance in locating and reproducing photographs in other collections. Elaine Goodman kindly shared drafts of her forthcoming biography of the African Art Museum's founder, Warren M. Robbins.

We are grateful to the Smithsonian Books staff— Carolyn Gleason, Caroline Newman, and Megan Miller—and to our outstanding designer, Robert Wiser, and editor, Diane Maddex of Archetype Press.

We are especially pleased that the proceeds of this book will go toward a restoration fund for the Smithsonian's buildings.

Heather Ewing and Amy Ballard

INDEX

Sacred
to the
Memory
of
James Smithson Esq.re
Fellow of the Royal Society
London
who died at Genoa
the 26th June 1829
aged 75 Years